TEDBooks

Beyond Measure
The Big Impact of Small Changes

MARGARET HEFFERNAN

TED Books

Simon & Schuster

New York   London   Toronto   Sydney   New Delhi

TEDBooks

Simon & Schuster, Inc.
1230 Avenue of the Americas
New York, NY 10020

TED, the TED logo, and TED Books are trademarks of
TED Conferences, LLC.

First TED Books hardcover edition June 2015

TED BOOKS and colophon are registered trademarks of
TED Conferences, LLC.

SIMON & SCHUSTER and colophon are registered trademarks of
Simon & Schuster, Inc.

For information about special discounts for bulk purchases,
please contact Simon & Schuster Special Sales at 1-866-506-1949
or business@simonandschuster.com.

For information on licensing the TED Talk that accompanies this
book, or other content partnerships with TED, please contact
TEDBooks@TED.com.

Interior design by: MGMT. design
Illustrations by: Hannah Warren

Manufactured in the United States of America

10 9 8 7 6 5 4

Library of Congress Cataloging-in-Publication Data is available.

ISBN 978-1-4767-8490-8
ISBN 978-1-4767-8491-5 (ebook)

For Pamela Merriam Esty

TABLE OF CONTENTS

I like what is in the work—the chance to find yourself.

Joseph Conrad

Beyond Measure

We measure everything at work except what counts. Numbers are comforting—income, expenditure, productivity, engagement, staff turnover—and create an illusion of control. But when we're confronted by spectacular success or failure, everyone from the CEO to the janitor points in the same direction: the culture. Beyond measure and sometimes apparently beyond comprehension, culture has become the secret sauce of organizational life: the thing that makes the difference but for which no one has the recipe.

The paradox of organizational culture lies in the fact that, while it makes a big difference, it is comprised of small actions, habits, and choices. The accumulation of these behaviors—coming from everywhere, from the top and the bottom of the hierarchy, from inside and outside of the company itself—creates an organization's culture. It feels chaotic and yet, at the same time, is susceptible to everything anyone does.

This represents both a curse and a blessing. For leaders, the curse lies in the sense that culture emerges of its own volition—not just beyond measure but also beyond their control. We may not be able to measure culture but we can measure the high rate of failure for programs aiming at culture change; that stands at around 70 percent. So the idea emerges that culture is elusive, hard to manage, impossible to command.

The blessing lies in the fact that institutional cultures are nonlinear systems. Small changes—listening, asking questions, sharing information—alter beyond measure the ideas, insights, and connections those systems are capable of producing. Each of these small things generates responses that influence the system itself. And everyone, from the CEO to the janitor, makes an impact.

That insight—that great cultures depend for change on small initiatives from everyone—has been central to at least one industry's transformation. When, in 1972, a British European Airways plane crashed three minutes after take-off, killing all 118 people on board, no single leadership change could address the scale of the tragedy. What made the disaster so bitter was the recognition that the crash had been caused by problems that many people had known about earlier, concerns that— had they been articulated—might have prevented the deaths. In the subsequent investigation, it became painfully clear that the failure to speak up, ask hard questions, or share concerns had been lethal. All the small barriers between people, functions, and geographies threatened the entire industry.

Yet from this disaster emerged a way of working together— building trust, sharing information and ideas—which, taken together, changed the culture of civil aviation. New routines were introduced that made it easy to raise concerns, ask questions, sound the alarm or share proposals. Where there had been secrecy, now there was openness. Where mistakes had been covered up, now they were acknowledged as learning, and widely disseminated without shame or blame. Where there had been deference, now vigorous contribution was invited and gradually emerged from all sides. This new way of working was called a 'just culture' and it transformed the least intuitive form of transport into the safest.

Today, we need just cultures across all our working environments, not just to prevent crashes but to draw from every single employee the best ideas, observations, concerns, and concepts inside every mind. We can't afford to let some thrive while others sit passively, demotivated or disenchanted. Our challenges are too big, the times too urgent, and the human capacity locked inside organizations too rich to let any of it go to waste. Just cultures tap the ingenuity, initiative, and sheer cleverness of every single individual; they reward imagination and celebrate truth-telling. They recognize that, while the road to success is littered with mistakes, it matters more to build trust and encourage ambition than to reward obedience. At the heart of any robust culture is an idea of leadership that isn't about second-guessing—markets, shareholders, stakeholders, bosses, and peers—but having the courage to think and speak for oneself and on behalf of others.

Because organizational cultures are nonlinear systems, they can't depend on just a few lauded superstars but draw their energy from the vast collective intelligence of every employee, affiliate, partner, and customer. In that, they're inherently democratic, demanding a generous and humble mindset. Information isn't cherished and held close to the chest because it represents power; instead it is shared and diffused for the inspiration and insight it provokes. If there is a single diagnostic indicator of a healthy workplace, it may just be the quality of connectedness and the ease of idea flow that characterizes them. In just cultures, every single person counts. As Randy Papadellis, the CEO of Ocean Spray put it, nobody wins unless everyone wins.

This sounds self-evident and it should be. But having run businesses both in the U.S. and in the U.K., I am staggered by the degree of passivity I see in companies around the world. I work with CEOs who are frustrated by the lack of energy and ingenuity they see in their workforce—while I talk to employees who feel equally frustrated by the rules and routines that constrain their thinking and deplete their initiative. I advise leaders immobilized by their belief that they are supposed to know everything—and I see their followers silent but wishing to contribute more. Everywhere everyone complains of silos, as though the last seven years of austere efficiency have left the barriers between people stronger than their connections.

I've lost track of the number of entrepreneurs I've interviewed who had what turned out to be a great idea—but which they hesitated to share, for fear of seeming foolish, out of line, off strategy, too wild, too pushy, too crazy. Passivity, articulated through silence, exacts a price not just when people feel they can't warn others about problems but also when they feel they can't challenge and explore new ideas. It's in that silence that opportunities—for redress or innovation—vanish.

In every country I've visited, locals have insisted this challenge is uniquely theirs. In Hungary, history is held accountable for a fear of speaking up; in Singapore, the desire to save face is implicated; in Latin America pride is the culprit; the Dutch hold Calvinist modesty accountable, while the British blame traditional reserve, and Americans describe themselves as conformist. From these and many more places, I've concluded that conflict aversion and a desire to please are universal, eviscerating our energy, initiative, and our courage.

When I talk to individuals about these wasted opportunities, they tell me the same thing: it's the culture. Culture has become the alibi, the scapegoat, for everything that is wrong. But who can fix it? Only everyone. That's why this book is aimed at everyone and anyone—from the CEO to the janitor—who wants a better place to work. It looks at the accumulation of small, everyday thoughts and habits that generate and sustain culture: ways of speaking, listening, arguing, thinking, seeing. These aren't multimillion dollar, multi-year programs; these are small steps that anyone can take at any time, the small steps that mark the beginning of big change.

What this book won't offer is a simple recipe for overnight transformation, the over-the-counter tips'n'tricks beloved of motivational speakers and corporate cheerleaders. Instead, there's a great deal in here about thinking: a rather prosaic, low-tech concept, easily forgotten and routinely underrated. But when we think, we have to stop what we're doing. If we let it, our mind will wander beyond cliché, jargon, second-guessing. That's when we find what we believe, who we are, and what it is we need to say. It's when we stop and think that we rediscover the courage, wit, compassion, imagination, delight, frustration, discovery, and devotion that work can provoke—in short, all the things at work that do count, beyond measure.

1 Creative Conflict

Imagine a room of twenty-one successful executives working for a global luxury brand. They're well dressed, well paid, well mannered, and well off. But that is their problem. They are so immaculate that they can't connect. So while on the surface everything looks and sounds fine, in fact not nearly enough is going on. The silence isn't golden; it's suppressed conflict.

Although the luxury of the company was unusual, nothing else about this scene was. Most people—from CEOs to janitors—would rather avoid conflict than embrace it. We fear our own emotions and we fear the feelings of others even more. So we develop habits and mannerisms to ensure that the argument never emerges. Psychologists call this "covering" and what it really means is that we obscure distinctive aspects of our personality, values, and passions when we come into work. In devoting so much energy to avoidance, however, we fail to move ideas forward; we get and stay stuck. But just cultures aim specifically at ensuring that conflict and ideas come out where they can be seen, explored, and confronted safely.

Scilla Elworthy can read the signs of silent conflict instantly. Three times nominated for the Nobel Peace Prize, she has devoted much of her life to developing effective dialogue between people who make weapons and those who want to ensure they're never used. The executives of luxury brands might not be her most natural constituents, but she has a lot to offer them.

"It was just a twenty-minute exercise," she told me. "They had to work in pairs, sitting opposite each other, in a comfortable place where they wouldn't be interrupted. The first person has to ask a nontrivial question—something like 'tell me who you really are' or 'what is it you most want from life?' For the next five minutes, their partner has to give the question their full attention, think about it with their whole body, heart, and mind, and report anything and everything they feel. Both have to maintain eye contact for the full five minutes. Listening must be inexpressive: no smile, frown, or expression should be allowed to steer the response. Then they trade places. And repeat."

What Elworthy described was a simple but far from trivial exercise. It demanded focus, concentration, and honesty. By formalizing the exchange, the detritus that mostly obscures dialogue in daily work was removed; small talk or second-guessing couldn't get in the way. Instead, each person had the experience—so precious in a working day—of saying what he or she truly believed and felt, and of being heard.

"We don't call it conflict resolution but conflict transformation. Buried under the dragon's foot is always a gem—something to be learned from conflict. And so you have to be able to name what is going on—and then to talk about it in a way that isn't explosive."

The experience proved so powerful that now, when the organization gets stuck, the team returns to Elworthy's process: they stop, sit down, and reconnect. The questions can escalate:

What do you love? What do you fear? What are your highest aspirations?

"The effect was so strong that it put our concerns in perspective," one participant recalled. "We became more real with each other. Fifteen minutes of that is worth four hours of discussion."

The purpose of a just culture is to surface all the information, intelligence, and insight required to make the best decisions. That means working in groups because, at its best, teamwork provokes the kind of constructive conflict from which better ideas emerge, honed by the clash of disciplines and the friction of divergent minds. And yet, when asked, most people will say that they are afraid of conflict and even fewer claim to like it. Leaders don't find this easy either, with 42 percent of CEOs acknowledging that the area in which they feel least confident is conflict resolution. Yet done well, it can indeed become what Scilla Elworthy calls conflict transformation: a positive process in which everyone grows.

Difference Makes a Difference

Truly creative conflict requires a complex array of personalities, backgrounds, thinking styles, and attitudes. But there are good reasons why this often does *not* happen. We are all biased. Our brain achieves much of its efficiency by searching for matches. When I see something similar to past experience, I take a shortcut and trust it, assuming it's roughly the same thing, and skip over any taxing new learning. But there's a catch. What is most familiar to me—is me. I'm the face I see in the mirror every day and the voice I hear all day long. So my brain prefers, feels

BURIED UNDER THE DRAGON'S FOOT
IS ALWAYS A GEM—SOMETHING
TO BE LEARNED FROM CONFLICT.

more comfortable with and confident in, people like me. That's why, statistically, individuals overwhelmingly choose as their life partners people who are roughly the same height, weight, age, background, IQ, nationality, and ethnicity. And it's why, as an ambitious young TV producer, when I sought to hire the best team I could find, I hired female liberal arts graduates who spoke several European languages, were under five-six and all had their birthdays in June: people just like me. Great teams need windows on the world, but biases mean that we mostly get mirrors.

This has been, of course, the rationale for several decades of diversity programs; teams do better when they consist of men *and* women. The most effective information networks include a broader range of people, backgrounds, expertise. And most companies seek to reflect the markets they serve. But if our biases work against us, how can we create and tolerate the diversity on which creative conflict depends?

Ted Childs knew how. I first met Childs at a diversity conference in London at the headquarters of IBM. These events were nearly always led by women, so I was surprised when an African-American man joined us. But when he started to speak, I knew why he was there.

Childs spoke of the experience of bias: its insidiousness, its invisibility, and the way that it was blind to itself and to talent that looked different. He described the battles he had waged inside IBM to implement policies that successfully attracted thousands of smart women who didn't leave when they had children but were supported and promoted throughout any careers they wished to pursue. Childs spoke with more authority on the subject of gender equality than anyone I had ever heard. Years later I asked him why he had been able to achieve so much. Was it because he was *not* female?

"Absolutely," he insisted. "Fighting for a group that is not yours is a completely different fight. When I got the diversity job at IBM, I was not going to lead with a focus on blacks. Women, the gay, and the disabled were my focus. That gave me my best shot at disarming people and getting them to believe that I am intellectually honest."

Childs was explaining what I'd felt that night in London: the unarguable moral authority of someone not out for himself. In truly creative debate, self-interest is always a liability, but selflessness is power.

Creative Conflict Takes Practice

Too much homogeneity makes rich conflict impossible. But so, too, does fear.

There's very little in most people's upbringing or education that prepares them for the ambiguity and uncertainty of heated debate. But that can be learned.

"You practice for auditions, for exams, to improve your tennis game," Brooke Deterline told me. "So why wouldn't you practice the kinds of arguments and conflicts that are bound to come up at work?"

Deterline works with companies on what she calls courageous leadership: teaching individuals at all levels of an organization to be able, calmly and clearly, to raise the issues, concerns, and ideas that they have at work. You could say that her whole mission is the reduction of organizational silence, teaching people to identify the moments at which they want to stand up and offer an idea or counterargument.

"One of the first series of programs that we did was at Google," Deterline told me. "Their value is 'do no evil.' The hard part is: how do we empower people to do good? Very few people come into work knowing how to do that or feeling that it is something they're allowed to do. So they have to learn and to practice."

A decade ago, aware that data privacy was bound to become an inflammatory issue, Google created a "Liberate" group that is passionate about protecting personal information. The data liberation group's fundamental function is to stop internal teams from imagining they can hold information captive. They have a specific remit to provoke debate because that's how the teams they work with stay honest.

Conflict in companies shows up in many guises. Sometimes it manifests as a rather polite ritual, of the kind that Elworthy found in luxury brands. Often it is contained in silence that represents a fear of stepping out of line—with good news or bad. And in many companies it hones in on trivial issues—food, parking—as a displacement for the substantial creative arguments that no one dares to initiate.

All of these conditions cry out for people with the courage, skill, and honesty to focus creative conflict on the issues that count. Books like Mary Gentile's *Giving Voice to Values*, Roger Fisher and William Ury's *Getting to Yes*, and Kerry Patterson's *Crucial Conversations* all demonstrate that however much people want to be open, they experience genuine difficulty living up to that ambition. All we have is a voice—and the time it takes to learn how to use it.

One participant in Deterline's program, Luke, had to stand his ground against a combative CEO who believed the only way to negotiate a contract was through intimidation and brute force—but this flew in the face of everything he believed in. So he worked through Deterline's simple prescription: he spent time thinking about the conflict, consulted his peers, and practiced his approach.

"I felt real pressure to act counter to what I believed was the right course of action," Luke recalled. "Before, I would have shifted automatically into conflict avoidance. But because we'd practiced these kinds of conflict, this time, I acted on my beliefs and secured the autonomy to run the remainder of the negotiation as I saw fit. Rather than losing sight of what I valued and giving in to pressure from the founder, I stood my ground, I met the deadline, and, working my way, I exceeded the financial goals for the project."

Recognizing that his values were at stake was a critical first step; when you're tired, distracted, or heavily focused on deadlines or targets, even that can be difficult. Experiments show that we often don't even notice the moral moment, and by the time we do, it's too late. But what Luke found was that identifying the moment at which he was tempted by silence made him stop to think about his choices. Advice, allies, and rehearsal gave him the confidence to stand his ground.

Whenever I talk to people who have resisted the urge to duck the argument, I hear the same story: "There was more give in the system than I imagined. And now I'll do it again." They come to see that articulating your values, beliefs, and ideas enriches work and turns what could be a sterile, soul-destroying confrontation into genuinely creative conflict. Or, as one executive recalled, "I began to see my whole professional life as an experiment, so much so that I began to welcome challenging situations—actually seeking them out—not only for my growth but for the growth of others and the overall health of my organization."

Crucial Differences

The German philosopher Hannah Arendt defined thinking as having a conversation with yourself. But for organizations to think, that conversation has to be with colleagues: testing, stretching, challenging observations, ideas, data, interpretations. The richness of the ensuing dialogue requires information and great questions.

Information wants to be different. If everyone brings the same knowledge, then why have five people in the room when you could just have one? Unanimity is always a sign that participation isn't wholehearted. Instead of seeking to confirm each other's biases and beliefs, why not bring data, stories, experience that enrich and expand? Great thinking partners aren't echo chambers—they bring well-stocked minds, new perspective, and challenge. Ask yourself: What do I have to offer that no one else can bring? That's what you are there for.

When Herb Meyer served as special assistant to the director of the Central Intelligence Agency and vice chairman of the CIA's National Intelligence Council, he was responsible for producing the US National Intelligence Estimates. But he grew increasingly uncomfortable with the data he received. As in most organizations, everything he was told just confirmed prevailing opinions: the Cold War was still going strong, the USSR was as powerful as ever. The lack of *disconfirming* data puzzled and unsettled Meyer. What if the prevailing wisdom were *not* true; what might the intelligence services expect to see?

I think Meyer's question is one of the best I've ever encountered for shaking up and enriching the exploration that should lie at the heart of critical decision making. What might we see if we were wrong? Meyer compiled a list of everything that could happen if the Soviet Union were collapsing and sent it to the spy networks. This was a low-cost experiment: if they saw nothing, then prevailing wisdom ruled. But one of the first pieces of data that came in was news of a weekly meat train that had been hijacked and all the meat stolen. The army had been called out—but then the politburo told the army to back off but tell no one.

"Well, that's not what happens when everything in the economy's just fine, is it?" Meyer asked. "You don't have people stealing meat and you don't have the army letting them get away with it. So that started to tell us something. And then there was more like that."

Meyer is widely credited with being one of the first people in the world accurately to forecast the collapse of the Soviet Union—not because he had a hunch but because he acted on it, sought disconfirmation, and had the courage and wit to ask a great question: What would we expect to see if we were wrong?

He didn't just sit on his concerns; he reached out to get the data and the allies he needed to challenge and change the conversation: conflict at its best.

Better Questions, Better Decisions

Questions are the heart and soul of constructive conflict. They open up the exploration, bring in new information, and reframe debate. When I attended London Business School, I compiled a book of questions because I realized that while the case studies dated quickly, the questions were perennial and could become habits of mind.

- Who needs to benefit from our decision? How?
- What else would we need to know to be more confident of this decision?
- Who are the people affected by this decision; who have the least power to influence it?
- How much of this decision must we make today?
- Why is this important? And what's important about *that*?
- If we had infinite resources—time, money, people—what would we do? What would we do if we had none?
- What are all the reasons this is the right decision? What are all the reasons it is the wrong decision?

Rich debate and argument are critical activities in any organization because, done well, they surface fears and doubts and they reveal ideas. They help us to see what we're prone to ignore, challenging us to think for ourselves, think better, think differently.

And this is critical at every level of an organization. Donna Hamlin coaches board directors on how to ensure that the right debates are had. Her rule of thumb: ask three questions for every statement you make. That keeps the conversation open.

For critical decisions, appoint a devil's advocate: someone whose specific task is to probe for disconfirmation, argue opposite positions, and surface data or arguments that have been trivialized, minimalized, or marginalized. No one should ever get stuck in this role—after a while, even the staunchest advocate will get tuned out. Revolving the role, however, presents a fantastic opportunity for critical, constructive conflict: an experience everyone needs to refresh his or her thinking.

The president of Pixar, Ed Catmull, vividly describes the ferocious Braintrust meetings that accompany the development of every movie. Debates are intense; arguments are heated; what makes them great at problem solving is candor. No one wastes time positioning remarks. Instead, everyone offers their best suggestions to a director who—crucially—is under no obligation to accept any of them. Some airlines put on their boards safety directors from their competitors, appreciating that peer-to-peer challenge is the best way to gain confidence on issues that count. Both are forms of collaboration in which experience, asking questions, listening, and long-term trust combine to get problems and original ideas out into the open.

Making the Most of Mistakes

Just cultures require that everyone bring their ideas, experience, attention, questions, and arguments to forge the best initiatives and systems they can. These won't be perfect; mistakes will be made along the way. But if people are too afraid of error, they won't be able to speak and think freely. Critical to the idea of just cultures, therefore, is the belief that as long as they are well-intentioned, mistakes are not a matter for shame but for learning.

At Massachusetts General Hospital, the orthopedic surgeon David Ring performed a carpal tunnel operation on a patient whose complaint was trigger finger. Only when writing up his notes did he realize his error and move, quickly, to correct it. But Ring wasn't content with that. He conducted his own, in-depth investigation of how he had come to make the mistake. And then he went one step further; he published his findings in the *New England Journal of Medicine* and became headline news.

Since then, Ring has become an outspoken champion for patient safety and the critical importance of sharing mistakes. "If you can't talk about mistakes," he told me, "you learn nothing. If anything, it convinces you that you're perfect—which is dangerous. If you can own up to mistakes, then others can, too. And that's how you learn. It's how whole organizations learn."

At Torres wine vineyard, there is a big black book. It isn't a list of disgraced former employees or disappointing suppliers. The Black Book of Torres is the book of mistakes. Whenever a mistake is made, the person who made it writes it up. One entry came from the chief financial officer, acknowledging a $200,000 error he had made in a currency hedge. But the value of the book goes beyond writing: every new recruit reads it on joining the company. So this simple book both shares the learning from the errors—so they aren't repeated—and sends a powerful message: everyone makes mistakes. Power and status confer no infallibility; mistakes are the way stations of progress.

Every decision is a hypothesis. Given the available information, a choice was made that will or won't deliver intended results in the future. When things turn out as we imagined, we call ourselves smart; when they don't, we call that a mistake. But really the hypothesis was just not proved. Being able to see that as new information, rather than error, turns debate into exploration, argument into thinking. Being able easily to say "I was wrong about that" removes the pressure to be perfect.

Most organizations pay lip service to the importance of mistakes—but few people believe it's safe to talk about them. In one recent study, of those questioned, 88 percent said they would address mistakes only in private; just 4 percent were willing to do so openly in front of others. But the correlation in medicine—between openness about errors and patient safety—is a compelling argument that openness about mistakes is what makes systems safer and smarter. How often, how easily, do you acknowledge when you were wrong? Doing so gives others permission to do likewise. Just as in aviation, highly complex procedures become robust only when everyone looks after them, takes responsibility, and cares.

Constructive conflict isn't a fight club and neither is it a social club. At Pixar, Ed Catmull says that in the beginning, all their movies suck. The same is true for ideas, doubts, concerns: they all start off roughly hewn, imprecise, and out of place. The first glimmer of an idea or an observation is like gold dust—highly cherished but hard to spot and not immediately valuable. We come together in groups and teams to refine, reshape, and polish them. The ensuing arguments are the signs that we care. It's through that conflict that the real luster starts to emerge.

2 Social Capital

Running a software company in Boston, I recognized—and my board told me—that we needed to reposition the business. Our product was too bland, too generic to stimulate excitement or loyalty. I needed a team to help me and ended up working through the problem with a motley crew: a young web developer, a seasoned and eccentric media executive, a visual artist, and myself. We spent a week, ensconced in the private room of a burger joint, exploring options, rejecting easy answers, pushing one another to find something none of us could see. Looking back, I recall that intense period as one of the most thought-provoking learning experiences I've ever had. The team was outstanding—and successful—but why? How did such an eclectic combination of people manage to work together so well? What made this experience of creative conflict so productive?

You could argue that we had a lot of brains in the room—and we did. But we also had something more important. We had social capital: the trust, knowledge, reciprocity, and shared norms that create quality of life and make a group resilient. In any company, you can have a brilliant bunch of individuals—but what prompts them to share ideas and concerns, contribute to one another's thinking, and warn the group early about potential risks is their connection to one another. Social capital lies at the heart of just cultures: it is what they depend on—and it is what they generate.

In a fascinating study of collective intelligence, Thomas Malone, together with a team of MIT researchers, analyzed groups that proved exceptionally effective at creative problem solving. Their goal was to identify the salient features that made some teams much better than others. What they found was that individual intelligence (as measured by IQ) didn't make the big difference. Having a high aggregate intelligence or just one or two superstars wasn't critical. The groups that surfaced more and better solutions shared three key qualities. First, they gave one another roughly equal time to talk. This wasn't monitored or regulated, but no one in these high-achieving groups dominated or was a passenger. Everyone contributed and nothing any one person said was wasted.

The second quality of the successful groups was social sensitivity: these individuals were more tuned in to one another, to subtle shifts in mood and demeanor. They scored more highly on a test called Reading the Mind in the Eyes, which is broadly considered a test for empathy. These groups were socially alert to one another's needs. And the third distinguishing feature was that the best groups included more women, perhaps because that made them more diverse, or because women tend to score more highly on tests for empathy. What this (and much more) research highlights is just how critical the role of social connectedness can be.

Reading the research, I can see my old team. We were all smart enough and had a wealth of different experiences, but no one deferred to anyone; that made us curious about what each could offer. We knew we needed an answer but we also knew that no one of us had it; we would have to work together to craft something we could not make alone. At times we were frustrated, scratchy, impatient. But nobody had any agenda. We all cared passionately about our shared success. In all of this, we'd been lucky; but can't we do better than luck?

Teaching Empathy

When I described Malone's research to a conference of five hundred business leaders, one asked whether it was possible to teach empathy. Did you have to hire for it—or could it be developed inside teams and companies? On the face of it, hiring for empathy—the ability genuinely to imagine how the world looks through the eyes of others—is fundamental. Customers and colleagues won't see everything as you do and sharing others' perspectives is how we learn. But none of us enters the workforce fully formed, and crucial skills always have to be developed.

Teaching empathy reminded me of Carol Vallone. She's now run three successful businesses, but when I first met her, she ran WebCT. The company was the result of the merger of her Boston-based, venture capital–backed business (originally called Universal Learning Technology) and a Canadian nonprofit. The cultural differences made Vallone confront the challenge of pulling a disparate bunch of people into a smart, functional team with empathy and respect that were not guaranteed.

When it came time to draw up the company's annual budget, each department head drew up a budget for that department—but then had to explain it so cogently to one colleague that the colleague could defend it at the leadership team meeting. The chief technology officer would argue the case for marketing, the head of sales spoke on behalf of operations, customer care explained technology's needs. The impact of this simple exercise was profound. Everyone had to see the *whole* company through eyes not their own. They felt duty bound to do the best job possible—if only to ensure their counterpart did likewise. They had to listen to everyone, not just wait their turn. In effect, Vallone was teaching empathy: getting each executive to see the company through the eyes of others and to appreciate the vital connections and dependencies between one another.

In large organizations, I've seen pairs of people choose to work out their problems this way. A functional head will challenge a regional head and then they will reverse roles. This way, they learn the exigencies and contingencies of both positions; they start to see common themes, ways they can help and support each other, and empathy grows. While many people recoil from conflict because they fear it will endanger their relationships, the paradox is that honest conflict—during the hard work together—makes social connectedness *grow*. When we avoid the argument, nothing happens. Only when we both engage in debate is our capacity to see each other's perspectives realized.

Mortar and Bricks

It's the mortar, not just the bricks, that makes a building robust. The mortar, in this context, is social capital: mutual reliance, an underlying sense of connectedness that builds trust. The idea of social capital grew out of the study of communities and what made them survive and flourish in times of stress. But the

concept takes on vital importance when applied to organizations that are now routinely beset by change, surprise, and
ambiguity. At work, no less than in communities, social connectedness plays a critical role in making individuals and
companies more resilient, better able to do conflict well.

Exploring and acknowledging the interdependence of her
department heads, Vallone's budget exercise built the bonds
that helped to make them willing to work together in search of
better ideas and decisions. High levels of social capital produce
trust of a kind that makes conflict safe, more vigorous, and
open. There's a virtuous circle here: creative conflict, done well,
generates social capital that, in turn, makes conflict safe and

constructive. (By contrast, an absence of social capital makes it impossible for people to speak and think openly—which means that they never develop the social connectedness they need from one another.)

Building social capital sounds like an abstract idea but it derives from an accumulation of small actions. When I talk to business leaders about this, many of them have reexamined small initiatives that fundamentally transformed their organizations. One told me about the silos of his business: geographical regions and technical functions found it hard to connect and trust one another. So he'd asked that each make short films about one another. He wasn't expecting anyone to invest much effort in the project but went to the trouble to gather the entire company in a cinema to watch what they'd made. The outcome startled him: movies of immense passion, inventiveness, and humor that delighted, motivated, and inspired the whole company.

"I didn't realize it at the time," he told me, "but I guess building social capital was what we were doing." Making the films meant the teams got to know one another; being in each other's films made them care about one another. Giving the activity a name made the CEO appreciate that getting people to invest time in the group was a fundamental business need.

Some companies now ban coffee cups at desks, not to protect computers, but to ensure that people hang out together around the coffee machine. ASE Global won't let employees eat lunch at their desks. In part, this is to ensure that everybody takes a break. But both policies create the opportunity for people to know one another.

"We had a nice lunchroom. But just having it wasn't enough," CEO Rob Jones told me. "We made it a rule so that people would see that we valued the value they find in each other. We think that matters to our business."

The Swedes have a term for time together at work; they call it *fika*. It's a moment when everyone gathers for coffee and cake, dispenses with hierarchy, and talks together about work and non-work. The word *fika* signifies more than a coffee break because it fosters a sense of togetherness. The Swedish researcher Terry Hartig calls this "collective restoration," arguing that the synchronicity is what gives the time its social and business value.

When Alex Pentland studied the communication patterns at a call center, he recommended that coffee breaks be rescheduled so that everyone in a team took a break at the same time. On the face of it, this didn't sound efficient, but providing that one opportunity to build social capital yielded the company $15 million in productivity gains—while employee satisfaction increased by up to 10 percent. Not bad for a coffee break.

I didn't know any of this when I started my first software company. We had gathered plenty of young, smart, energetic, motivated people who all worked furiously. But everyone was so focused on tasks and targets that there was little give-and-take. Everyone worked hard, but they worked alone. Even in the first year, turf warfare threatened: engineers thought marketers made too much noise, and accountants thought salespeople were awfully expensive for people who were always absent. Work was being seen, and executed, as a transaction; the relationships between people weren't growing.

What I devised was so simple I still feel awkward writing about it. On Friday afternoons, we stopped work early, got together, and listened as a few people told the whole company who they were and what they did. Some used PowerPoint—others performed sketches, wrote songs, or told stories. We learned about one another. An engineer had worked on one of the first Internet browsers, a marketer had devised a famous tagline, a Russian designer had taken huge risks to leave her home country. You watched respect grow. Ten years later, the same process in a completely different business yielded similar results; work between people became more direct, open, and fearless as executives came to see human value in one another and to gain trust. Social capital grows as you spend it. The more trust and reciprocity you demonstrate, the more you gain in return.

Work at MIT has quantified this. Alex Pentland's team tracked the patterns of communication of teams in a wide range of organizations from hospitals to banks to call centers. They discovered that those patterns of interaction were as important as everything else (individual intelligence, skill, personality, the contents of discussion) *combined*. What happened between people—not just at meetings but in casual conversations, brief exchanges in the hallway, at the water cooler—made a measurable difference in productivity. And his tracking quantified what we've all felt—that the real influencers of an organization are the network nodes: the people who most often intersect with the most people. Their titles may not signify power, but that's what they have—and it is through them that social capital compounds and change accelerates.

Time Compounds Social Capital

Within academic circles, the scientist Uri Alon is famous for breakthroughs on the boundary between physics and biology. But he is more widely acclaimed for a 2010 paper "How to Build a Motivated Research Group." (Scientists are closely akin to entrepreneurs in the sense that success hinges on identifying hard problems and solving them—often in a race against time.) Alon knows time is precious but he still devotes the first half hour of his weekly two-hour meeting to "nonscience": birthdays, the news, the arts. This might appear to reduce the time for real science—but in the long term, Alon says, the gains from increased motivation more than make up for the losses. When the group moves on to discuss science, he assigns each member a different role—as imaginary referees or brainstormers—which helps to structure the constructive conflict within the lab. All of this, he says, builds the social connectedness on which every scientist will rely when they hit the difficulty and confusion that always accompany scientific breakthroughs. For Alon, social capital is what makes those discoveries possible.

Investing in the connections among team members both increases productivity and reduces risk. The National Transportation Safety Board found that 73 percent of incidents occurred on the first *day* a team worked together, and 44 percent on the first flight. By contrast, flight teams that stayed together for years performed better than all the rest. The late Richard Hackman's research into teams showed that superior teams tended to be very stable; they work together for a long time, getting to know and trust one another. Switching people in

THE BENEFIT OF LONG-STANDING TEAMS

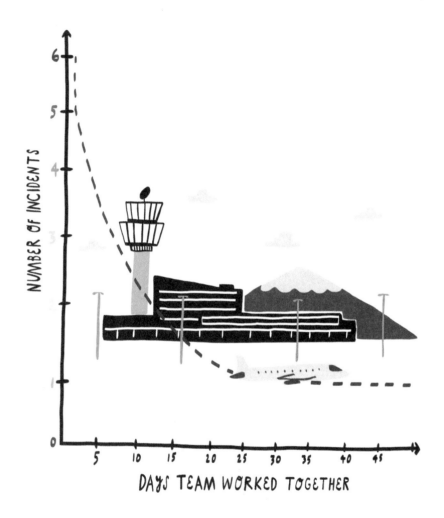

NUMBER OF INCIDENTS

DAYS TEAM WORKED TOGETHER

and out didn't make them more creative—it was disruptive and dangerous: newness was a liability. Shuffling roles within a stable team produced enough change, while preserving the value of familiarity that develops from working together over time. Even in research and development, where new talent is needed to refresh ideas and knowledge, Hackman concluded that the introduction of just one person, every three or four years, would suffice.

Without high degrees of social capital, you don't get the vigor of debate and exchange that hard problems demand. Creativity requires a climate of safety, but without social capital, no one will risk the fresh thought, the unpredictable idea, the testing question. That even the finest talent needs social capital became clear when I heard a CEO describe an organizational failure.

He told the story of a hugely gifted executive who had been transferred from Hong Kong to the European headquarters. Everyone had had high hopes for him—but after he arrived, he floundered. Disconnected from his team, deprived of social capital, his intellect alone was insufficient—yet when he returned to Hong Kong, he was again a superstar. Remarkably, the CEO concluded that the individual hadn't failed—the organization had. It had failed to appreciate the degree to which IQ alone isn't productive; it needs support, safety, candor, connections, and trust to thrive.

Social capital isn't about chumminess. It doesn't mean work colleagues have to become best pals or that good cheer is a permanent requirement. Many of the greatest teams are scratchy, sharing an impatience with anything less than the best. Grumpy orchestras tend to play better than cheerful ones; they're focused on performing better and happiness is the output, not the input, of their work together. In organizations with high degrees of social capital, disagreement doesn't feel dangerous, it is taken as a sign that you care; the best thinking partners don't confirm your opinions but build on them. They know that every idea starts out flawed, incomplete, or downright bad. In organizations with high degrees of social capital, conflict, debate, and discussion are the means by which it gets better.

Building social capital makes organizations more productive and creative because high levels of trust create a climate of safety and honesty. That makes companies more efficient and profitable, too. How? By making it easier to ask for help. Helpfulness may sound like a rather anemic quality, but studies of teams across industries as varied as paper mills, banks, pharmaceuticals, and retail all demonstrate that the helpfulness of a group has a direct impact on profits, costs, productivity, and efficiency. Helpful teams of people accelerate the sharing of knowledge and expertise; they don't let one another stay stuck or confused; they try to prevent problems before they arise and they won't let colleagues become isolated or cut off. Social capital compounds even as we spend it. And the longer groups work together—the more social capital they accrue—the more these benefits grow. Trust, helpfulness, practice, and courage become the simple renewables that power our working lives.

Power Listening

Try this experiment. The next time you attend a meeting, promise yourself you won't say a word. This may sound simple, but listening requires courage—it means you have to be open to what you hear.

Many executives regard this experiment as some kind of torture. They're used to meetings where they go in with prepared arguments they're determined to land. They listen for nothing but the perfect moment to jump in and shut down debate. But building high degrees of social capital requires as much listening as talking. The equality of contribution that Malone found so important only becomes truly dynamic when you bring the courage and the humility to both talk *and* listen, and to be open to change.

In the Quaker religion, listening is considered a way of deeply experiencing the present. Meetings are seen as representative of a distributed mind, and the silence of listening isn't a failure of communication but a form of social support. Eoin McCarthy, a consultant who is also a Quaker, is often asked to sit in on board meetings and to raise a red flag when he hears a decision being made. He told me that individuals in meetings are often so intent upon their own contribution that they don't notice when they close off avenues for debate.

McCarthy has become a professional listener. So, too, is Matthew Owens, conductor of the Wells Cathedral Choir, one of the finest church choirs in the world.

"It's more important to be able to listen than to make a sound," he told me. "In singing, you have to listen to each other—and respond. The best ensembles listen and respond; it's the responsiveness that makes them distinctive."

When Owens listens, he's highly attuned both to the whole—the space, the mood—and to the individual performers. You need, he says, a second set of ears. As a conductor, Owens does what many of us could do in meetings: listening for mood, encouraging what works and lifting the tone before it flattens, fine-tuning pace and progress. He fully appreciates that what makes a group unique is its capacity to listen and to generate a fresh response.

The more senior you are, the more important listening becomes. Once a leader speaks, most people stop listening to one another and start positioning themselves. But when the leader doesn't speak, then, just like a great choir, people have to listen to and respond to one another. That's how and when distinctive work emerges.

Scott Cook, the founder of Intuit, listens for surprises: the comments or data that contradict or challenge his assumptions. Sheryl Connelly, who runs the global consumer trends division at Ford, writes down anything she hears that she disagrees with or is surprised by. She's also fastidious in taking notes; reviewing them often draws her attention to details she hadn't appreciated in the heat of the moment. I try to listen for what is *not* being said and am keenly interested in the emotions of the group and how far anyone responds to them. I doodle a lot; it helps me to keep my mouth shut—and there is some evidence that doodling helps you to retain what you hear. Some groups I have worked with take turns appointing a listener—not quite an umpire but someone whose role is to listen for subtext. No one who has ever taken this role comes away thinking it's the easy option. Some even chart the discussion, with one column for what is said—and another for what it means. It's a simple way to unpack contradictions, fears, unspoken truths.

Listen. Leave time to think. Truly respond to what has been said—not with the argument you prepared earlier. And don't interrupt. This last, simple habit is hard for many people to develop but profoundly changes pace. We interrupt when we think we know where an argument or a sentence is going—but our interruption blocks new ideas or thoughts. Moreover, when participants know that they won't be interrupted, the mood of the meeting changes. Urgency, the fight for airtime, dissipates. Knowing you will be heard creates space for thinking.

Just cultures depend on social capital to create the sense of commitment and safety that keeps people listening, talking, and thinking through all the frustration, confusion, doubt, revelation, and discovery that creative conflict necessarily generates. But just cultures also compound social capital by taking it seriously, recognizing that the dynamic between people is what brings organizations to life.

3 Thinking Is Physical

My business school students occasionally get to watch TV. It isn't a treat. I show a clip from a financial news channel—Bloomberg, CNBC—and ask them to retain as much as they can. With scrolling subtitles full of stock prices, a right-hand box of weather forecasts or sport scores, there's little space left for the hapless CEO breathlessly explaining quarterly results. When the clip ends, I ask what anyone recalls. A few prices, tomorrow's temperature in Barcelona, the CEO's company's name—that's about it. When I ask for a critique of the corporate strategy, they are dumbfounded: You mean we were supposed to follow all that information *and* think about it? But that's impossible!

It is impossible. Higher-order thinking—argument, skepticism, doubt—is cognitively expensive, requiring more of our brain's capacity. The brain's resources are limited and attention is a zero-sum game. When you pay attention to one thing, you have less for everything else. Avid concentration on scrolling data leaves little cognitive capacity for analysis. We may imagine that we can multitask, but no brain is built to do so. Just cultures rely on and reward the highest levels of attention and creativity that we can muster. But distraction, fatigue, and overwork profoundly, quickly, and inescapably undermine these. Culture may feel abstract, but the just culture absolutely requires that the physical demands of work be respected and understood.

Monotask!

Trying to do everything makes multitaskers poor editors. Those who consistently attempt multitasking find it harder to ignore irrelevant information and take longer moving between tasks—in other words, for all their frantic activity, they're actually wasting time. And because the brain's competing memory systems store information differently, whatever is retained is harder for the multitasker to recall. While these energetic minds might feel that they're on top of the world of information, in reality they are at its mercy.

So how we work creates its own feedback loop: the more attention we try to pay to everything, the less discerning we become. But when we focus, we get better at concentrating—and remembering what we did. We feel less exhausted. So monotasking—focusing on one task at a time—isn't only more efficient; it also leaves us better able to use the knowledge we have gained. This isn't just a matter of productivity. Distracted people can't think, which also means they cannot begin to think for themselves. They may make good sheep, but they will never make great leaders.

Engineers talk about asset integrity, by which they mean that systems and machinery must be looked after, serviced, and repaired before anything goes wrong. At industrial sites, asset integrity is the cornerstone of safety, efficiency, and sustainability. But for those of us who don't work with physical machinery, the machines we use are our brains, and we need to appreciate their limitations as fastidiously as any site engineer. We mostly don't do that—but we could.

Hours Up/Productivity Down

In 1908, one of the earliest productivity studies, conducted by Ernst Abbe at the Zeiss lens laboratory, concluded that *shortening* the working day from nine hours to eight *increased* productivity. Subsequent studies throughout the twentieth century, across industries and countries, have all reached the same conclusion: productivity isn't linear. We can work well for forty hours a week but no more than that. After forty hours we get tired and make mistakes—so we need extra time to clear up the mess we've made.

Industries such as aviation and transport have long paid serious attention to fatigue because when people driving planes, trains, and trucks crash and kill people, it's impossible to ignore. But industries where disaster isn't so visible or immediate have proved recalcitrant. Working through the night is heroic; long hours are interpreted as commitment. When companies fail or big deals don't deliver (mergers and acquisitions have a failure rate of 40 to 80 percent), nobody stops to consider that exhausted brains might be the culprits.

The problem isn't that we can't keep working when we're tired; we can. But exhaustion and distraction create tunnel vision that the Chemical Safety Board explains like this: "It is common for a person experiencing fatigue to be more rigid in thinking, have greater difficulty responding to changing or abnormal circumstances, and take longer to reason correctly." Tired and overwhelmed, we want problems to go away—we don't care how—because we lack the capacity to analyze or solve them. With a bad case of tunnel vision, what are the chances of correctly identifying an error, perceiving a solution, or coming

THE NEGATIVE IMPACTS FROM WORKING LONG HOURS.
HOURS WORKED

up with a good idea? Virtually nil—all you're trying to do is get through the day.

In 2012, the Finnish researcher Marianna Virtanen built on a forty-year study of public servants to examine the long-term impact of working long hours. What she found was startling. Working eleven or more hours a day had at least doubled the risk of depression. Those working fifty-five hours a week or more began, in midlife, to suffer cognitive loss. Their performance was poorer when tested for vocabulary, reasoning, information processing, problem solving, creativity, and reaction times. Such mild cognitive impairment also predicted earlier dementia and death.

Fatigue is an operational risk, implicated in almost every industrial accident. Sleep deprivation exacerbates the problem. The brain needs seven or eight hours of sleep a night. Deprived of that, the loss of cognitive capacity is roughly equivalent to being over the alcohol limit. Parts of the brain that manage information (primarily the parietal and occipital lobes) become less active while the area of the brain responsible for keeping us awake—the thalamus—becomes hyperactive. This makes sense in evolutionary terms (if survival demands food, staying awake takes priority over creative menu design), but for critical thinking, it's disastrous. Moreover, after twenty-four hours of sleep deprivation, less glucose reaches the brain, and that loss isn't shared equally either: the areas we need for thinking lose most. We may feel heroic working through the night, but the machinery we bring to our task is badly—sometimes dangerously—compromised.

Waking Brains

The brain you take to bed is not the same as the one you wake up with. While being very tired and lacking sleep demonstrably reduces our ability to think clearly, it also deprives us of the benefits that sleep bestows. My father-in-law, a scientist, has been known to solve equations in his sleep; I once cracked a fairly simple code that way. Mendeleyev, the father of the periodic table, claimed to have gleaned its underlying principle in a dream. More recently, Larry Page says the idea for Google came to him in a vivid dream. Jeff Taylor says the same about founding Monster.com.

These examples aren't flukes. When we are asleep, our minds are busy, consolidating, organizing, and reviewing recent memories and experiences—and that generates insights. In experiments in which participants have to organize information that appears random but is in fact presented according to a complicated underlying rule, those who've had a good night's sleep proved *twice* as likely to figure out the pattern as those who have not. Sleep, the researchers concluded, inspired insight. The restructuring of information that takes place asleep allowed participants to see what otherwise had eluded them.

What is so striking about over a century's research is that long hours specifically impair the talents we most need in business today: thinking, insight, problem solving, sharp analytic and imaginative skills. Distraction and fatigue deeply compromise our ability to test our decisions, reflect, and think again. Without the capacity to doubt, we will never gain the confidence we need to ask hard questions and articulate the values that define us. It is rested and subsequently focused minds that prove productive and resilient. Time is on our side when we know how to spend it.

Quiet Time Together

When Harvard's Leslie Perlow studied the usage of time in a software company, she asked engineers to log how they spent their time. The results are sadly familiar: an early start full of good intentions waylaid by interruptions and meetings, "real work" didn't get under way until late in the afternoon. Out of the twelve hours one engineer spent in the office, he thought only five and a half had been productive—and those had been at day's end when his brain was already tired.

Perlow had the insight to appreciate that not all of those interruptions were unproductive. People asked for and got help. The engineer was updated on critical changes and also took a break to make his draft pick for Fantasy Football. Ideal working days wouldn't eliminate these. The social and intellectual capital they built was valuable. The problem was the impact of the interruptions.

The logs revealed two kinds of work, described as "real engineering" and "everything else." You don't have to be an engineer to appreciate the difference; all our working days could be divided into real work—which takes concentration and quiet—and the social interaction of meetings, taking or giving help, and jokes and gossip. To be truly productive we need both. What drives us mad is that we don't feel in control of what happens when—or where.

Perlow designed an ingenious experiment. What would happen if the schedule reflected the two different kinds of work, divided into separate parts of the day? Quiet time would be a designated part of the day in which engineers could work alone, confident that they would not be interrupted—because everyone else would be doing quiet work, too. The rest of the day would be available for "everything else."

Quiet time was set three days a week, from morning until noon. The engineers loved it. Some reported that their productivity had increased by as much as 65 percent. The smallest thing—reengineering time—had made a dramatic difference. For only the second time in the company's history, a product shipped on time.

At the beginning of the experiment, the quiet time system was challenging. Engineers had to learn to prepare for the quiet time—to plan ahead to ensure they assembled the information they needed. Now that they appreciated how disruptive interruptions could be, they learned to be more considerate. "The quiet-time study made me think about how I am impacting others," one engineer noted. "I realize now that it is not just a pursuit for my own quiet time, but others' quiet time must be considered. It has made me more aware of others' needs." And a colleague wrote, "People have begun to respect others' work time. The focus has moved from themselves to the team. Interruptions still occur, but people take the time to think about what they are doing before interrupting. They are more prepared."

This didn't mean that they asked for or received help less— in fact, they became more helpful, confident that the "real work" had been done or that they had time safely available for it. Knowing that the time needed for concentration was protected freed everyone to be more generous the rest of the day.

People crave the time to focus on their most important tasks and they can learn to use time well. Just being able to prioritize tasks—becoming a good editor of what your brain attends to—can increase productivity by more than 50 percent. Those who can clear significant blocks of time for focus get more done faster and feel less stressed doing so.

Moreover, synchronizing the time during which work gets done yields tremendous benefits. It gave the engineers a strong sense of autonomy: they had control over their time that their managers respected. Quiet time reduced multitasking and enabled focused work to get done without incurring social and intellectual costs. It built social capital by teaching people to consider the needs of others.

When I've discussed quiet times with companies, many managers are aghast at the prospect of losing their right to interrupt; those who report to them, by contrast, typically look thrilled. But the prospect of delivering on time without exhaustion has encouraged many to experiment with the idea. The consultant Tony Schwartz once persuaded an accounting firm to let just one group work differently, alternating focused, uninterrupted periods of ninety minutes with short breaks. That group stood out from their peers as getting more done in less time, being able to leave earlier and experiencing less stress during tax season.

Other organizations have implemented some variant: At Ocean Spray, there are times in the day and the week when no one can call a meeting. That simple rule provides freedom in scheduling work or external commitments. The Pohly Company designed big, pretty "Do Not Disturb" signs for cubicles and chairs: an easy, individual way to win focus. Other organizations I know have quiet rooms—places without phones where no one is allowed to interrupt you. "I don't always work in there," one heavy user confided in me. "Sometimes I just think. Or breathe. Or try to figure out what to do next." I'd call that work, too.

Creating the conditions in which the best work is most easily achieved is the job of any leader of any group of any size. But even if you don't work in an organization where big changes such as quiet time feel feasible, you can think about how you organize your own time. When I worked as a television producer, I made an appointment with myself—every Thursday from eleven o'clock until twelve thirty I would leave the office and go somewhere I knew I wouldn't be interrupted. This was my thinking time, often the most productive of the week.

Giving myself the time to do "nothing" allowed my mind time to wander. Inevitably, I'd remember critical information I'd overlooked. Or I'd suddenly see a simple solution to a problem that had had me stumped. Because I travel a great deal, I now make it a rule to devote time to staring out the window. I can't always get as much time off as I'd like, but I can use the interstitial moments—going from one place to another—to switch off. Horizon scanning is good for my eyes and my brain. No music, no screens, no podcasts, no radio. Whether I'm on a plane or a train or the back of a car, this enforced leisure is where and when real thinking happens. And it has turned tedious travel into a retreat.

Wanderlust

The act of thinking may be what makes us distinctively human and it clearly underlies the creativity, innovation, and productive work on which organizations rely. But that doesn't mean that people readily choose to think or that they find it pleasant. In a recent study, 83 percent of adult Americans said that they spent no time at all "relaxing or thinking"; moreover, when invited to do so, they didn't enjoy it.

Yet allowing your mind to wander can prove an effective way to solve problems or gain new insights. When we focus too hard on our work, we can become fixated, inflexible, and unreceptive to new patterns, people, or ideas. When we look away from work, we access other parts of our brain that help us find the information or pattern we need for understanding or resolution. To be truly productive, therefore, means to take time for quiet, focused work but also to find time to let your mind wander.

Many people have experienced the revelation that comes in the shower, while driving home from work, or while cooking dinner. Activity that is automatic (or at least undemanding) frees the mind to do unconsciously what has eluded the conscious mind. And that's not just anecdotal evidence; controlled experiments likewise show that creativity is enhanced when we take a break and do something simple. Of these, one of the simplest, cheapest, and most effective is walking.

Whether outdoors or on a treadmill, walking has been shown to improve the generation of new, useful ideas. While physical activity generally enhances thinking, walking in particular increases creative output by around 60 percent. Walking outdoors appears to produce the greatest number of new ideas while also restoring previously exhausted cognitive capacity. Before brainstorming, when you're stuck with a problem, or just because you need a break and some exercise, taking a half hour walk can prove wildly more productive than staying late at work.

For your mind to wander, you need time alone. The CEO of a major global bank once told me that in the past five years, he'd spent just one day alone; the aftermath of the financial crisis had eliminated all his thinking time, just when he needed it most. But how can you know what you think if you don't have time to think without interruption? How can you move beyond received wisdom and stale assumptions without solitude? If you are going to be able to explain your ideas and thoughts, you need time to explore them first. First thoughts are rarely best thoughts; you need time to wander beyond them. Time alone need not mean introspection—there are better subjects to think about than yourself—but it does mean making room to explore doubts, challenge your own assumptions, and hear weak signals. If you have a conversation with yourself, you had better listen.

Crunch—Then Detox

None of this is to deny that there aren't times when critical deadlines or opportunities make it essential to move into crunch mode. The term derives from the software industry, where it's

... Than STAYING LATE AT WORK.

routinely used to push a product over the finish line. Everyone works late, and there's frequently a great sense of camaraderie being in the trenches together.

Crunch can be great—as long as it doesn't last forever. In 2004, software teams working for the computer games giant Electronic Arts started by doing eight-hour days, six days a week. But that quickly turned into twelve hours six days a week, then eleven hours a day, seven days a week. Crunch had become standard. Watching what happened to her fiancé who worked there horrified the blogger Erin Hoffman; her public outcry eventually resulted in a class-action suit against the company. "After a certain number of hours, the eyes start to lose focus; after a certain number of weeks with only one day off, fatigue starts to accrue and accumulate exponentially. Bad things happen to one's physical, emotional, and mental health. The team is rapidly beginning to introduce as many flaws as they are removing. The bug rate soared in crunch."

Since the lawsuit was settled in 2006, Electronic Arts has ameliorated its scheduling—but other companies have gone further still. SAS Institute, a leader in the field of data analytics, allows its people to work for thirty-five hours a week and no more. The reason is simple: the work requires clear heads and real concentration, and thirty-five to forty hours is the human limit. In a tough and competitive industry, limiting working hours hasn't constrained the firm's success but made it sustainable.

Crunch can become addictive. Yet, as with any kind of addiction, you choose your form of detox. Some executives I know build into their working year a very sizable chunk of time—a month, sometimes more—when they stop working altogether. Others who lack that freedom become more disciplined about vacation, commitments that they deliberately make too hard (or expensive) to cancel. Daimler employees are encouraged to delete any e-mails received when they're on leave, leaving automatic messages saying they're doing so. Volkswagen turns off e-mail outside of office hours, while the Huffington Post urges workers not to check e-mail outside of work. But everyone I ask, from the C-suite to the reception desk, talks about using weekends as recovery time. Evgeny Morozov's solution is perhaps the most extreme—he locks his laptop and cell phone into a safe with a timed combination lock so that, however twitchy he may feel, he cannot access the Internet until Monday morning. His mind has time to wander elsewhere.

I make it a rule that in the summer, I read only fiction. Most of the year, I don't have time for novels or short stories and my reading tends to be utilitarian. So I shift gears by making myself read books that require a different mindset and pace. I do this because I enjoy it but recent research suggests that it is beneficial in more specific ways than changing pace. Reading fiction—excerpts from National Book Award finalists, winners of the Pen/O. Henry Prize for short stories, or even Amazon bestsellers—has been shown to enhance theory of mind: our capacity to appreciate the difference in other peoples' minds. In one experiment, participants were given the same Reading the Mind in the Eyes test that Tom Malone had used in his study of teamwork and empathy; those that had read just three pieces of literary fiction did better—and literary quality made a difference.

Throughout our working lives—one hundred thousand hours—time is our most precious asset. Once spent, we can never retrieve it and we can never manufacture more. So deciding how to spend it is powerful. When it comes to time, most organizations are very good at measuring its quantity but poor at measuring its value. We need time for quiet, focused work. We also need time to let our minds wander and find the insights and inspirations no amount of focus will ever bring. Synchronizing time for a team, a project, or an entire organization can create a powerful sense of community. But walking away from work can be the greatest contribution we make to it.

4 Smashing Barriers

Tod Bedilion is a curious man. A senior director at Roche Diagnostics in California, he has spent his working life in biotech, first at start-ups and today at Roche, one of the world's leading pharmaceutical companies. A typical corporate scientist, you might think. But you'd be wrong.

"I've always been curious—about everything. What we do, how we do it, why we do it. And that has made me increasingly frustrated with the way that we do research and development. But I'm not alone; we surveyed about 250 R&D leaders and they shared that frustration. The two biggest obstacles to innovation were rigid hierarchies and not getting enough from the skills that we have in this company."

It isn't just research units that suffer. Every company I've ever worked with complains of rigid thinking, a lack of creative vitality in the workplace, and a failure to collaborate across silos. Just cultures aim to get more from everyone inside them. But doing so requires that however coherent the internal culture, it remains open and receptive to the world outside. So there's a paradox: for the culture inside to be vibrant, it has to let the outside in.

Curiosity Smashes Silos

Bedilion and his colleagues devised an experiment. First, they identified six challenges—current problems from mechanical engineering to biochemistry—and broadcast those across all 2,400 members of Roche's R&D community. The response disappointed Tod: only 419 employees even looked at the challenges and only forty submitted proposals, some of which were no more than a few lines. But one netted a winner: a way to measure battery life in glucose drip meters. But this proved a bittersweet victory. The problem had been set by the diabetes care team in Germany and the engineer who solved it worked on that team, too—but in Indianapolis. And this was the first time he'd heard about it. It just showed, Bedilion reflected, how intelligence gets trapped and hidden by organizational structures.

By contrast, one of the toughest challenges, which had defeated Roche for twenty years, was also broadcast to 160,000 "solvers" working on an open innovation platform called InnoCentive. This time, the response astonished Bedilion: 113 proposals packed with detail, data, diagrams, experiments, and energy. After sixty days, with a cash reward of just $25,000, one novel offering cracked it.

Two hard problems had been solved. But some Roche researchers were hostile to the experiment and its results. Bedilion was passionate about new thinking, but many colleagues resented the notion that anyone *outside* had anything to offer. "The hackles came up, the feathers came up," Bedilion recalled. "They were quite defensive about *other people* solving their problem."

The experience showed him how easily talent becomes constrained: hard to find, siloed, disconnected from the outside world and one another. Organizational structures create division and we internalize barriers: departmental demarcation lines, geographical boundaries, corporate pecking orders, and technical prowess. Expertise itself can inhibit innovation because it typecasts people, narrowing what they think about—or allow themselves to think about. Everyone gets mentally stuck on their square of the chessboard.

"The InnoCentive system is great," Bedilion explained. "But finally this isn't about technology. Or geography. It's about mindset. Are you mentally rooted to the confines of your job—or does curiosity send you crashing through barriers? You need to keep that core curiosity—to be open and enabling. Walk around. Talk to people. Turn the other cheek. Build a network. Feed that network. Don't get boxed in."

It's striking that many of InnoCentive's successes come from solvers working outside their specialty. The search for a biomarker for ALS (Lou Gehrig's disease) was aided by a plant biologist and a dermatologist. The Oil Spill Recovery Institute (OSRI), still trying to find better ways to clean up the Exxon Valdez oil spill of 1989, sourced a critical solution from a cement engineer. These solvers had the curiosity and the mental freedom to work wherever they chose.

The Roche experiment wasn't a contest between the company's R&D and InnoCentive's open platform. Both solved high-order problems. But the experience illustrates the bigger challenge: How can our workplaces embrace, connect, and enliven *all* of its talents? How do organizations realize the benefit of assembling a concentration of gifts in a single place? The counterintuitive answer is: Let them roam. Don't nail them down. Mentally and physically set them free.

MENTALLY, EVERYONE GETS STUCK ON THEIR SQUARE OF THE CHESSBOARD.

Heads Out: Get Out of the Office

Seeking to tear down the mental walls that constrain thinking and collaboration has inspired most companies to tear down office walls. Seventy percent of US companies now use open-plan offices and hot desking in the hope that these free-form physical structures will provoke free-form thinking. This architectural determinism isn't entirely convincing—there's plenty of evidence that people find open workspaces noisy, distracting, and impersonal. Walking through several such workspaces recently, I couldn't help but notice how hard everyone was working to simulate privacy. Plugged into headphones, surrounded by stacks of books and temporary dividers, defensiveness was more evident than openness.

Architecture alone won't change mindsets and tearing down physical walls won't demolish the mental silos that trap thinking. For that, you need to escape offices and immerse yourself in life.

"I led a billion-dollar business line and people often think that all you need to know, to understand a business, is found in the numbers. Nothing could be further from the truth—because the real meaning of the business lies elsewhere."

Louise Makin was ambitious and eager to sustain the growth of Baxter International's biggest business: treatments for hemophiliacs. But she soon learned that the numbers couldn't show her what mattered.

"It was only when I started going out to patient associations that I understood. I met a mother with her son who had just been diagnosed with hemophilia. They needed us massively and would depend on our products for the rest of their lives. Would we keep supplying old products? Would we develop new ones? Were we big and bold enough to keep investing in the business? You couldn't see it just as a business anymore; you were right into a life. It changed my whole perspective."

That experience, Makin told me, shifted her approach to developing and positioning the drugs. Instead of thinking about transacting, she thought about collaborating with patients and families to develop the therapies they needed. Today, Makin is CEO of BTG, a health-care company that focuses on highly defined areas of medicine—liver disease, blood clots, varicose veins. That narrow remit allows deeper relationships with patients and physicians. BTG doesn't see doctors as hapless targets to be bludgeoned into buying; salespeople aren't the only ones who meet doctors. Adopting a sailing term, Makin calls this "heads out" and argues that in any new work, you always have to have at least one person who is nominated to stay heads out: scanning the horizon, staying in constant touch with the wider environment.

Introduce Divergent Thinking

At Roche Diagnostics in Switzerland, Matthias Essenpreis put together what he called "a very weird team" to lead a new development in the company's diabetes diagnostics strategy. All earlier products had worked in hospitals and intensive care units, but now the company wanted something that patients could use themselves. This shift in perspective inspired Essenpreis to reach across Roche and bring in diabetics who worked for the company. But then he went further, bringing a visual artist, Kelly Heaton, into the team.

"I needed a radical outside view," Essenpreis told me, "a person who has no experience with Roche or diabetes but a holistic thinker, a truly unconstrained thinker. The team was so excited by what she could offer that we brought her in full-time. She had this great skill—in asking the right questions with anybody. She maintained a vision. This was a very intense period when no one could leave the room or finish a day without a discussion that excited people and we made a real breakthrough in understanding."

For Essenpreis, this experience proved the most creative time of his career. Today, as chief technology officer of Roche Diagnostics, what he prizes most highly is the opportunity to liberate and connect people.

"Typically with rigid structures you get silo thinking. Instead now what I care about passionately is connecting different people *across* those unnatural boundaries. That's how you make the silos disappear—because the nodal points where those boundaries intersect are the most creative."

Much the same approach was found, almost by accident, at ARM, which now designs the processors powering most of the world's smartphones and tablets. How has it, from small beginnings in Cambridge, England, grown to be a powerhouse of innovation and design? According to Tom Cronk, the general manager of the processor division, it has been by tearing down mental and physical barriers between ARM engineers and the companies they work with.

"The business model evolved through necessity. We were just twelve people and we had a big opportunity to serve an equipment and manufacturing business that had ten thousand employees! The only way that could possibly work was for *us* to become part of *their* team. Being territorial was not an option! And that's how we've worked ever since. Very few people at ARM don't have contact with partners. We have desks—we just don't spend much time there. Most of our people are working inside partner organizations."

Over time, many organizations develop managerial narcissism: an obsession with the internal workings of a business that takes attention away from the market and their customers that inspired it. At ARM, the relationships with the outside world are so fundamental to the business that that—not corporate headquarters—is where many of their engineers, architects, and designers live and work. Whereas many organizations talk about divisions, what Cronk is talking about, and Makin and Essenpreis experienced, is a porous membrane—between the company and the world. It is their interaction, their frequent collisions that make the businesses creative.

"I couldn't say whether it's that we go out, or we let them in, but either way, there's just no real boundary between us," Cronk observed. "That's the power of the business model. Our engineers here feel, act, and think the same whether they're talking to one another—or to partner engineers halfway across the world. It isn't about control. We trust them a lot."

Driven by curiosity and characterized by a striking absence of defensiveness, these organizations want their people to be highly comfortable out of the office and in the world. Companies such as iRobot and the UK broadcaster Dave build simulations of their customers' homes inside their offices as reminders of where their customers live. Other companies get their executives to take turns playing the customer. But nothing beats getting out of the office and being with the people for whom all the work is designed.

GO: Get Out!

InnoCentive uses technology to draw in ideas and energy from as far afield as its network can reach. BTG and ARM build rich external collaborative networks to the same end. Essenpreis introduced a completely different mindset by including a visual artist. All these approaches smash through the formal constraints of work to expand insight, talent, language, and energy. Preserving—or reviving—innate human responsiveness reflects their appreciation that great ideas don't come from offices but from life.

"I have an old friend, Jim, who is a glass artist. He makes beautiful pieces that sell for around two thousand dollars. And when I was catching up with him, he told me he'd just missed out on a sale: a woman who only had a credit card and certainly not enough cash."

The glass artist's friend was Jack Dorsey, one of the founders of Twitter. But his success didn't keep him in the office. It gave him to freedom to roam.

"The conversation left me thinking, why couldn't Jim handle the credit card payment? His problem made me think about all those people—at craft markets and farmers' markets—who probably had exactly the same problem. So how could I solve their problem?"

This is how Dorsey came up with Square: a small plug-in for smartphones that turns them into credit card readers. By 2014, the combined sellers using Square represented the thirteenth-largest retailer in America. Dorsey's new idea hadn't grown out of Twitter, from a focus group, or out of market research. It had grown from life. Without his friend, without the experience of markets, without their collision with Dorsey's technological expertise, his friend might still be losing sales.

In order to build a rapid prototype of his idea, Dorsey turned to TechShop, a workshop open to the public, that's crammed full of machinery—welders, water cutters, 3-D printers, looms, and lasers. Over the last twenty years, technology has made these machines cheaper and easier to operate than ever before. But it isn't just the tools that make TechShop such a creative space. When you join, the understanding is you can ask anyone for help—and you must help anyone who asks you. From the outset, founder Jim Newton and CEO Mark Hatch envisaged it as the preferred playground of inventors, artisans, and entrepreneurs, a physical innovation platform where collisions were bound to happen.

When TechShop opened in Detroit, Ford Motor Company provided two thousand free memberships to employees who submitted good ideas. Anybody in Ford could apply and their ideas didn't have to relate to cars. But access to tools, machinery, and expertise from all over Detroit—not just Ford—lured employees from all parts of the business. After one year, the company credited TechShop with a 50 percent increase in patentable ideas by its workers.

Put down your cell phone and look around. Be where you are. It's from the real world that ideas, provocation, and pattern recognition come. No one ever had a great idea at a desk. Walking is creative but walking outdoors even more so. The breakthrough that led to the polymerase chain reaction technology and kickstarted the genetic revolution didn't come from a conference room but from driving down a highway. Many CEOs say their leadership training comes from coaching Little League. Great engineers routinely talk about their best inventions stemming from hobbies. From a business perspective, engaging with the world is your best, fastest way to tune in to the mood of the moment, of the markets that you serve. And from a human perspective, being in a rich and open community is how you build and enrich the neural networks of your mind.

School friends Eric Ryan and Adam Lowry used to get together regularly to compare notes about trends they observed, hoping to identify a business to build together. Early in 2000, they noticed that people were spending more time and money than ever on their homes—but cleaned them with products that were toxic, smelled awful, and were so ugly they had to be hidden. What about creating cleaning products that honored the planet, were fragrant, and were so beautiful that they'd be kept out on display? That positioning led to Method home care products, a business that would never have been possible without Eric and Adam being out in the world, alert to its moods and passions.

Even after the company's success, Ryan and Lowry have remained obsessed by keeping the company open and responsive to the outside world. Because Method won't use toxic chemicals, it can locate the entire business (including R&D) not in a business park but in the center of downtown San Francisco. Everyone takes turns manning the reception desk, being the face—and interface—of the company. Eric sits right next to Meghan who answers the company's 1-800 customer service line. He wants to hear what people call about, what worries them, what questions and ideas they might have. Meghan attends product design meetings so that her conversations spread, so that the outside permeates the company's thinking.

Around a hundred employees—people against dirty—are spread across a number of sparklingly clean, expansive rooms crammed full of desks, prototypes, and whiteboarded walls. Cocreation here is everyone's job. There are walls covered in whiteboards where anyone can add ideas and insights. But the spirit of collaboration on which the company depends isn't just about architecture. It derives from a sense that everyone counts and everyone contributes. The founders work hard to ensure that everyone feels connected to everyone else, not trapped in hierarchies they can't breach. As a consequence, on entering any of these rooms, you can't tell who's a founder and who's an intern.

The people against dirty talk easily and openly about mistakes they've made; there's no defensiveness here. Eric and Adam seem keenly aware of how much they don't know, how much they will always need to keep learning from the world around them.

Autodesk offers opportunities for employees to swap lives—exchanging jobs, desks, even homes with colleagues in other towns and countries. Arup encourages employees to work on projects around the world, building technical expertise and social capital across the forty-two countries in which the engineering firm operates. Most companies, sooner or later, insist that executives visit the clubs, pubs, stores, or malls where their customers spend time. Many companies encourage volunteering and some specifically reward people for the breadth of their involvement with groups outside of work. All of these initiatives have the same goal: to make the mind travel well beyond the desk, beyond the conference room, to build new neural networks that refresh thinking and make new connections.

Making Offsites Work

In building what became Boston Scientific, John Abele became mildly obsessed with collaboration. What made it work, why did it so often not work—and what were the conditions that might make it easier? For most companies, offsite meetings are the occasions when this becomes critical, when people inside and outside the organization come together to tackle hard problems. But too often, these attempts at creative collisions reinforce mindsets instead of resetting them. Hotels look a lot like offices; rooms and suites have hierarchies, too. Seating reflects pecking orders and it's easier to talk to the people you already know. Those dismal experiences inspired Abele to try to create a setting for offsites that would be different.

"I liked Kingbridge because it was a pink elephant architecturally," Abele told me. "It is easy to get confused about where you are. There's a lot of space (different types of hallways) for transitioning from one state of mind to another. There's a lot of wall space for art and contrasts from one microenvironment to another. I think of walking through the mirror or closet, Narnia style. There are many spaces that enable creative theater that involve music, light, and more. That makes it possible to surprise guests while also giving them a sense of comfort and personal, friendly attention."

"John wanted, when he bought the place, to create a different kind of space," Lisa Gilbert told me. She now manages the center after a disillusioning career in a hospitality industry she no longer found hospitable.

"In traditional hotels, you get different sizes of room. He wanted none of the rooms to be different: no premier spaces, no presidential suite. It's about leveling the playing field. He also wanted to create a space that is more social. The dining room isn't like a restaurant, it's like eating at home. You see barriers coming down and people stay talking for hours. John never wanted this place to be designed by a decorator—each area is imperfect, with furniture that looks like home. You can just wander around; people don't hide out."

Creating a climate of comfort and safety is a deliberate attempt to make Kingbridge offsites feel as different from work as possible. "We take people out and get them to be playful and have them see new things in a fun, gamelike way. If they can be different outside the meeting, they can be different inside the meeting. It's about building the courage to explore."

Kingbridge deliberately sets out to unsettle established routines and behaviors. Changing the rules of working life can have the same effect. One of the best conferences I attended took a unique approach to team building. Over the four days, every attendee (including CEOs and presidents) had to do a kitchen shift and a serving shift. You could find yourself being served by a former prime minister or cooking alongside the head of an NGO. The message was clear: everyone here has a contribution to make and everybody counts.

Go Home

With the advent of the Industrial Revolution, work that once had been done at home became centralized in offices and factories. These developed unique architecture, furniture, jargon, rules, and behaviors. This made them very efficient. It also turned them into islands. The financial journalist Gillian Tett points out that in London, the financial district in Canary Wharf *is* an island. Its geographical and mental isolation from the rest of the world was one reason financiers were so blind to the risks they ran. Likewise, lavish campuses that serve every human need are efficient but risk becoming narcissistic bubbles, cut off, self-referential, and defensive.

Many organizations are jealous of time spent away from them, regarding work as serious and home as trivial. This is a profound error. Home enriches work because it demands a shift in perspective. Its difference is its value. One Procter & Gamble product manager once described his first experience of having a part-time worker on his team. He'd been hostile at first but the experience changed his mind. "What I found," he told me, "was that it was incredibly valuable having someone who wasn't *here* all the time—who was out, in stores, in homes, talking to families, in all the places and in all the relationships we should speak to."

But home offers more than market research. It can be a place where hierarchy falls away, where challenge can (and should) come from anywhere. Arguments at home, with people you can't easily fire, prove a fantastic training ground for listening to and mediating competing interests. Home is where our values are most present, most active, remind us of who we are and who we want to be. As such, it offers time for reflection and a rich testing ground for our ideas and beliefs.

The anesthetist Stephen Bolsin struggled for years because he worked alongside a dangerous pediatric cardiologist. Operations took too long, recovery was compromised, children died. Bolsin found little support from his colleagues; hospital leaders didn't want to know. The temptation to give up and shut up was immense. But one night, as he described his difficulties to his wife, their conversation was overheard by his five-year-old daughter. She walked over to him and said, "You can't let the babies die, Daddy." Seeing his predicament through the eyes of the powerless gave him the energy he needed to persevere until standards were changed.

If you have children, home can also be a vantage point on the future. If the business community is routinely criticized for its short-termism, then seeing the impact of decisions on the next generations can be an eye-opening antidote. Never mind what you're delivering to your shareholders: What are you creating for the future that sits across from you at dinner?

Always uncertain of the future and ignorant of its demands, our greatest resilience lies in well-stocked minds, undeterred by barriers, constantly replenished by new people, experiences, and the ideas that they spark in us. Engagement with life isn't a rival but a partner to the work. Enriched by experiences broad and deep, with minds free to focus or to roam, we find what we need to say—and the courage to say it.

5 Leaders Everywhere

In a classic piece of psychology research, a primary school teacher and a professor teamed up to study how far expectations drive outcomes. To do so, they administered IQ tests to California pupils in grades one through six. Teachers were told that certain pupils—around 20 percent—showed great promise and could be expected to make exceptional progress. At the end of the year, that forecast proved true: the IQ of the nominated pupils showed superior improvement. But, like all great social psychology experiments, this one had a catch. The "high-potential students" had been chosen at random. What came to be known as the Pygmalion effect argued that it is expectations, more than innate ability, that influence outcomes. Never mind who's gifted, who's talented. Expect great things and you are more likely to get them.

The talent, energy, insight, and opportunity of any organization lies with its people. They are where all ideas come from; they are its best early-warning system. All of the risk and all of the opportunities lie in the workforce. In just cultures, no one needs permission to be creative or courageous. But they do need support, encouragement, and belief.

The Elevating Impact of High Expectations

After the Pygmalion experiments were published, subsequent researchers couldn't help but wonder whether the same effect might be observable in adults. Could you make teams more productive just by expecting more of them? Two Israeli researchers—Reuven Stern and Dov Eden—studied a thousand men in twenty-nine platoons. Stern met with all of the platoon leaders and explained that it was possible, on the basis of test scores, to predict the command potential of the soldiers. And, to particular platoon leaders, he broke the news that their group's tests indicated exceptionally high potential. No individual soldier was singled out; it was the group as a whole that showed promise. Once again, the platoons described as high-potential had been chosen at random.

Sure enough, those groups nominated as exceptional turned out to be so: raising leaders' expectations of their men caused performance improvements of at least 20 percent. Moreover, "the Pygmalion effect is not a benefit enjoyed by some at the expense of others. It is a boon that can be shared by all." Nobody had to fail for the others to succeed.

No one in these groups started out unfit for service, disgruntled, or disengaged, so there was a baseline of commitment and fitness for the work. But the study challenges organizations everywhere to consider how they assess and manage talent. Résumés, interviews, psychometric tests, and behavioral profiling are routinely recruited to identify talent and potential. But nominating some executives "high-potentials" may be no more than a self-fulfilling prophecy. Give these individuals special attention, training, and support and of course they do well. But it's worth considering the message conveyed to the rest: you don't have potential.

Forget Forced Ranking

Many organizations disable much of their workforce by apply-
ing processes that confer the opposite of the Pygmalion effect.
Of these, the most prevalent is forced ranking, an exercise
every six or twelve months in which a workforce is assessed and
segregated into one of three camps: the supertalented 10 to 20
percent, the bottom 10 to 20 percent, and all the rest. You don't
need to be a mathematical whiz to perceive that in this system,
there must be far more losers than winners. Those in the top
group love it because they are confirmed as leaders, talented,
and full of possibility. Not surprisingly, they tend to live up to
this expectation and to feel responsibility for the organization
that has so clearly identified and articulated their value.

But the rest? The bottom group is explicitly encouraged
to disengage and leave—some managers have called this a
kindness. But those in the middle group—the majority of the
workforce—are completely stuck. Few at the top wish to mentor
them because doing so jeopardizes their own elite status. Peers
are reluctant to help and support each other for the same reason.
But perhaps most telling of all, the segregation of the "best"
sends a powerfully demotivating message: they're leaders,
you're not. The advancement of the few comes at the cost of
passivity and apathy in the rest. This is not, of course, the intent,
but it is the consequence. Why care about a system that doesn't
appear to care for you?

Most of the world's largest companies rank people, hoping
to co-opt their competitive instincts and drive them to higher
levels of performance. In reality, the system disenfranchises

the majority of the workforce and sends out a costly message: you are not a leader. With Pygmalion in mind, you might call this the Galatea effect—taking living human talent and reducing it to stone.

Most organizations invest more in rooting out underperformers than in cultivating pervasive achievement. Standard tools of appraisal, assessment, and ranking provide an illusion of control, a comforting defense against the slacker. But they've overengineered the solution to the small problem while ignoring the bigger one. Turn that around—focus instead on liberating and celebrating talent—and the results are predictably disproportionate.

Forced ranking creates a visible and felt hierarchy, which discourages helpfulness and accountability, precisely the qualities most valuable in creative collaborative organizations. It specifically devalues social capital. So it was a telling moment when a bellwether that had long cherished ranking chose finally to abandon it—which is what Microsoft did in 2013. The new CEO, Satya Nadella, now sees it as critical to the company's mission to do everything in his power to foster a different kind of ethos, dubbed "One Microsoft," where everyone—not just the top few—feel active, invested, and responsible.

"Culture," Nadella said, "is everything. That's why I try to meet all our new graduate hires. They are our lifeblood! And I keep beating the drum—management is here to serve the workers. We have to get people at the bottom not to take any bullshit. We have to be in touch with all of them. We have to get the best from everyone."

The symbolic power of eliminating forced ranking was lost on no one. Nadella faces a bigger challenge: how to excite and motivate every single person in a vast company full of bright, ambitious individuals. He isn't alone. Most global businesses today have initiated programs that go by names such as One Bank, One Store, and One QBE, all of which aim to align all of the talent within them, to demolish silos and fiefdoms and to liberate the talents of every single employee. It could be simpler than many realize.

Leaders Believe

When Google launched a data-mining program to determine the characteristics of their best managers, many involved in Project Oxygen expected technical expertise to head the list. But out of the top eight qualities, that one came last. What mattered most to people was working with colleagues who believed in them, cared about them, and took an interest in their lives and careers. Most striking of all, they preferred managers who would help them to puzzle out problems themselves—not by giving answers but by asking questions. Supplying answers shuts a conversation down and implies superiority, but asking questions, as a way of solving the problem, implies confidence: you can crack this, you just need a little support. Once again, questions trump solutions and social connectedness proves highly motivating.

Believing in the people who work with you proves effective because it gives them the confidence to persevere in the face of difficulties. In doing so, they develop a sense of self-efficacy. The experience that shows them they can succeed. Being trusted, they learn to trust themselves. People who are helped by a system are more likely to take responsibility for it. Support, help, mentoring, and leadership become richly reciprocal.

When executives believe that expertise and omniscience are all that matters, they edit out their concern for people around them. I knew one brilliant manager who cared deeply about his team members, their families, their professional and personal hopes and dreams. But he never let that show, thinking it trivial. Once he changed, the response was phenomenal. Treated as whole human beings, his team brought more of themselves to work: all their energy, all their imagination, all their ideas became available. What the Pygmalion experiments and the Google data demonstrate is that one of the simplest ways to elicit great work from people is to show you believe in them. This isn't about chumminess; it is about seeing the depth of the people you work with. See them. Know them. Understand them. Show you care. Take time to do this. It sounds simple because it is.

All of my working life, companies have routinely restructured, reengineered, reorganized themselves in an effort to unlock energy and ideas. This always involves eliminating individuals who are euphemistically described as "dead wood." But were they dead to begin with? Did the company recruit and hire dead people? Of course not. But lack of time, attention, and concern had killed off the interest and talent with which they'd begun.

Distributing Power

When I described forced ranking to the engineers of Arup, the look of puzzled amazement on their faces spoke volumes. They understood the concept readily enough—they just couldn't imagine how it could be productive. Arup is one of the world's most successful architectural engineering firms. Its credits include the Bird's Nest stadium in Beijing, the Cheese Grater in London, the longest bridge in Australia, and a bioreactive facade in Berlin, constructions at the cutting edge of human ingenuity. In its sixty-nine years, the company has never lost money, borrowed, or shrunk. Terry Hill has worked at Arup for over thirty years. He says that much of the firm's success has always depended on minimizing hierarchy.

"Before I started with Arup, I'd worked with contractors who always had a rigid hierarchy. But here, I was trusted, just allowed to get on with my work. When I came back from my holidays, the guy I had been working for offered to work for me. He'd been my boss on my first job—and now I was his boss on my next job!"

At Arup, such flexibility isn't unusual. Teams are formed according to the expertise that the job demands—and the skills that individual engineers seek to develop. One engineer, Hill told me, moved from doing high-rises in London to sustainable development in Africa. She wanted to learn new skills, and helping her achieve her aims enhanced the firm's capabilities. Success at Arup isn't about climbing a ladder but building a diffuse infrastructure rich in leadership everywhere.

"We don't recruit to fill vacancies," Phil Hood told me. "We don't really even have job descriptions. We're good at looseness. There's a lot of discipline and process in *what* we do but we try to keep *how* we do it as responsive as we can."

Sharing lunch with a team of Arup engineers is unlike the experiences I've had in other companies. It isn't just the un-prompted eagerness with which people talk about their work or the delightful absence of media training in their conversation that stands out. What they're describing and the way they talk about their work match. The subjects flow effortlessly between people according to who has most experience or insight. Instead of hierarchy, what I'm watching is heterarchy: an informal structure that changes in response to need.

Central to the idea of heterarchies is the belief that everyone matters. Just as the human brain itself is not hierarchical—its different areas and capacities are recruited in different com-binations according to the task—so, in creative organizations, every individual counts. Instead of rank indicating importance, in great teams you want everyone to feel that they matter. Respect flows from capability, not position. Once you work from the simple assumption that everyone counts, everyone contrib-utes more. This doesn't mean that everyone does everything—knowledge, expertise matter—but leadership is fluid.

The Best Idea Leads

Everyone counts. At companies such as Morning Star, the world's leading tomato processor, they use different words but the idea is the same. No one has titles, ranks, privileges. Instead, the mantra is: knowledge is the leader. Just as at Arup, the leader—of a project or a problem—is the person most able to come up with the best solution on that day. At Gripple, a British manufacturing firm, the same spirit prevails. The CEO sits amid the rest of the staff and the only job description is simple—if the ball's falling, catch it. Jim Henson used to invite the janitor to meetings. The absence of hierarchy, of formal job descriptions and rankings is deliberately designed to make everyone feel responsible and to bring their best.

On one of my visits to Arup, I asked the engineers what, with offices all over the world, would I see that would tell me I was in an Arup office?

"You wouldn't be able to tell who was a director and who wasn't," one said. "All of the offices are different. But in any one of them, you'd see people working around tables and you'd have no idea who was the boss."

Hierarchies make it easy for a few to have power and the rest to defer or check out. But in organizations that strive to reduce pecking orders, everyone is encouraged to see themselves as leaders, capable of being and making others successful. That's the point at which an organization approaches the holy grail of teams, mutual accountability. Where I feel that I can succeed, among people I know, trust, and care for, why would I let them down?

The Power in Powerlessness

In 1989, the Montreal Protocol required the phasing out of all CFCs, the chlorofluorocarbons shown to be responsible for the hole in the ozone layer over Antarctica. CFCs were big business, used in refrigeration, aerosol sprays, cars, and many manufacturing processes. So the race was on to find a new way to create a substitute that could quickly replace the banned chemicals. At age thirty-nine, the managing director of ICI's fluorochemicals division, Geoff Tudhope, faced an enormous challenge, not least because he lacked expertise.

"I'm not a chemist or an engineer; I have a law degree," Tudhope told me. "So I had to be very careful about giving direction. I knew we had good people and a good track record in this area. But I had to lead from the human side."

Together with his head of engineering, Frank Maslen, Tudhope knew that the scale of the chemistry challenge, coupled with the unprecedented urgency of the timetable, meant that the company would be forced to think and work differently.

"We didn't know if we could do this—no one knew," Tudhope recalled. "But Maslen came to tell me three things. First, he said, what I want to try is this: No stars in this team. We are all just scientists. Nobody stands tall, everyone has a valid point of view. And second, we work to just one standard: the best imaginable. Then he added the final thing. He told me I had to butt out."

Tudhope got the message. He knew that when it comes to innovation, power can prove disruptive and destructive. And he shared Maslen's view that the urgency and scale of the challenge was so exceptional that not a single voice, talent, or idea could be wasted. Everyone had to count. Tudhope's role was to hold the team to its principles.

"I watched the team's body language to see if everyone did get their say. I would sit in meetings, just as an observer, and listen. Did anyone look marginalized or sidelined? Was anyone silent? But they weren't. Even the women—we had a number of female scientists—were right in there! So much energy, such sincerity. From every one of them."

Without technical expertise, and declining the power to intervene, Tudhope wasn't doing nothing. He protected the team by holding them to their own standards of trust and candor and by reporting progress to his bosses, thus ensuring the team's freedom. High trust with low levels of interference produced an exhilarating result. The Montreal Protocol—the most successful international environmental agreement ever implemented— had called for the elimination of CFCs by 1996. Tudhope's team delivered their alternative in 1994.

"We cracked the new technology ahead of every competitor including DuPont, gained forty percent of the US market from zero, and were recognized by the Royal Academy of Engineering with the MacRobert award in 1993! It was a pretty remarkable achievement of trust, teamwork, and the excitement of daring to have the standard of the best imaginable. Amazing learning opportunity for me, too."

The Problem with Power

"I believe that the more power you give away, the more you have, because when people are trusted and empowered they take ownership and will not let you down," Paul Harris wrote to me. "I judge management not by the number of people they control but the number they liberate. My attitude is that I have never learnt anything from someone who agrees with me so I expect *everyone* to talk openly to me even if their opinions differ from mine or those above them."

Harris is the former CEO and cofounder of FirstRand bank in South Africa. Although he is a wealthy man, his favorite topic of conversation isn't money or status. What fires him up is bringing people together as equals. He doesn't think people work for him. He works with them.

FirstRand is known across southern Africa as an innovator and a trusted resource. As early as 2000, the bank introduced an electronic payment system that brought buyers and sellers together, and it pioneered the use of cell phones for banking transactions. Such innovation, Harris insists, depends on the freedom and talent of the entire organization. Talking with Harris, you can't help but feel that his commitment to human equality is deeply personal. But he also appreciates that steep hierarchies are hard to operate; it's difficult for information to flow from top to bottom, while second-guessing the powerful proves an elaborate and wasteful game. That's why Geoff Tudhope agreed to butt out of the search for a CFC replacement—he knew status could derail exploration.

We may think of power as a prize or a privilege—but it's a problem, and the steeper the hierarchy, the bigger the risk. Many of the rewards of power are, in themselves, isolating: the private jet, first-class cabin, limousine, or corner office is circumscribed by walls, not porous membranes. And power changes people.

Powerful people who control resources tend not to pay much attention to the less powerful. In experiments, they are less able to see the visual, cognitive, and emotional perspectives of others and, as a consequence, may make less accurate judgments and form relatively shallow understanding. More recently, brain imaging has shown that those with power are less responsive to others. The paradox of power, therefore, is that while we need leaders to show that they care about others, they often can't.

"I guess I could ask their opinion," one COO grudgingly conceded to me. Frustrated by the lack of coherence and energy in his global business, he knew the answers he sought lay within the bright people around him. He rated them and knew they cared. But he didn't feel he could ask for help. Leaders are supposed to know all the answers, aren't they? His sense of himself—that as a leader, he was supposed to be omniscient—trapped him under a burden he couldn't shift alone.

Like a great idea, power is at its best when given away. Asking for help could have enlisted all the bright young minds this COO wished to engage, smashing the hierarchy and silos that immobilized him. As Geoff Tudhope found at ICI, the more power you give to the people *around* you, the more likely it is that they will step up to burnish a bright good idea or to illuminate an incipient risk.

While much in our culture celebrates leaders as heroic soloists, most CEOs recognize how fully they depend on the people around them to stand up, speak up, and reach deep down inside their organizations to surface the critical people and information they need. We may imagine large organizations are run single-handedly by charismatic, uniquely gifted geniuses, but truly creative, adaptive, and relevant companies don't concentrate power on top floors or top people. Even the icon of the superstar CEO myth, Steve Jobs, turns out not to have been the sole source of the company's design mastery.

"The biggest misconception is this belief that the reason

Apple products turn out to be designed better, and have a better user experience, or are sexier, or whatever . . . is that they have the best design team in the world," according to former Apple designer Mark Kawano. "But *everyone* there is thinking about user experience and design, not just the designers. And that's what makes everything about the product so much better . . . much more than any individual designer or design team. The reason that structure works isn't because of a top-down mandate. It's an all-around mandate. Everyone cares."

Lead from Where You Are

Hierarchies create chasms across which people gaze, uncertain how to connect. On one side are managers, feeling alone, cut off, and isolated by the burden of power. On the other side stand individuals full of ideas, knowledge, insight, and energy. They're waiting—for permission, for a sign that it's safe to stand up, reach out, forge ahead. I'm not sure, they tell me, whether I should do anything. Nobody asked me to. I'm not a leader. It's not my job . . .

It might not be your job, but it is your life. Most people will spend around a hundred thousand hours at work. That's a long time to be stuck with ideas that find no outlet. Even when you're working in a steep hierarchy, there are small ways to disrupt it, to make space for your contribution. One of the most hierarchical work cultures in the world is medicine. It's well understood that medical school education contains a "hidden curriculum" that teaches a pecking order in which a senior doctor's decision must always carry the day, even when it's wrong. That long, difficult, expensive education, coupled with high pay and high stakes, puts doctors on a pedestal, but it's dangerous for patients when a bad senior decision can trump a smart junior one. It is for that reason that checklists were invented.

During major operations, the adoption by major hospitals of simple checklists was found to reduce deaths and complications by more than one-third. In part, this was because they reminded often fatigued physicians of critical details. (They typically require that everyone know their colleagues' names before a procedure begins; not a high degree of social capital but better than nothing.) But their true power lay in the fact that they disrupted hierarchy—it didn't matter how junior or senior you were, the checklist prevailed. It's not unusual for the responsibility of managing the checklist to be given to the most junior member of a team. This tiny mechanism—because it represented a schedule of agreed requirements—took the deeply entrenched, traditional power structures of a hospital and tossed them out the window.

Doctors developed the checklist with help from colleagues in the aviation industry, who in turn had inherited it from W. Edwards Deming, a statistician working in Japan in the 1950s. Focused primarily on manufacturing businesses, Deming argued that barriers between staff had to be removed, that fear should be driven out, and that annual rating or evaluation systems should be eliminated. The message Deming sought to convey was simple: *No one should have to ask permission to take responsibility.* Checklists enact that principle. Checklists take power from the few and disperse it among the many. They give each person a mandate.

Hacking Away

All companies have crises, moments when their ways of working no longer seem relevant or effective. Most companies respond in one of two ways. Either the CEO withdraws to figure out, usually alone or with just a few trusted subordinates, a whole new structure and vision that are then cascaded down the steep hierarchy. Or external consultants are bought in to craft a solution, in the hope that their objectivity (or ignorance) will impart fresh thinking to old problems. In both scenarios, a few exceptional beings are loaded with unwieldy hopes and expectations and routinely fail.

But nobody is committed to an organization like the people who work there. Every day they see things that could be done better—or not done at all. In the software industry, hackathons emerged as a process by which large numbers of programmers were brought in to collaborate furiously, over a short period of time, to design or improve new products or platforms. And that process is now used to address any kind of system. When John Lasseter, at Pixar, thought the company had become too unwieldy and expensive, he launched a hackathon to garner ideas that he now says revitalized the company. In 2011, the US government ran a hackathon to garner ideas for improving federal agencies. Similarly, schools have launched them to improve curriculum and scientists to bring different disciplines together. In Britain, local communities have created hackathons to determine the future of their towns. The goal is to focus as many minds as possible for a limited period of time on a specific issue, challenge, or problem. They're fast, furious, and, in a strange way, fun.

It is critical that hackathons are structured, specific, and practical. Typically, they focus on a defined business problem, e.g., costs, use of time, culture. Groups work together—sometimes physically, sometimes virtually—to thrash out practical proposals that address the issue. Time is always limited and participants choose what to work on. Senior leaders may structure the hackathon but they don't participate; the goal is an exuberant openness that allows ideas and insights to be traded fast and furiously. At the end of a day or two, each group presents practical proposals they are prepared to champion personally.

At the last hackathon I attended, an entire business unit stopped work for a day to work on itself. Before getting together, everyone had suggested topics and ideas, many of them posed as great questions: Why can't we? What if we could? Each hour they changed groups until, by day's end, they had tackled the same challenge from multiple angles with colleagues from all over the company—many of whom they had never spoken to before. What emerged was a broad and deep agenda for change: practical, original, with energy and commitment behind it. In a day, the organization went from grumpy, inchoate, and discontent to a revitalized sense of achievement and possibility.

Many companies—Pixar, Publicis, Grant Thornton, Leeds Teaching Hospitals NHS Trust, FactSet—use hackathons as a means of reaching deep into their organizations to find insight and ideas. They reduce internal rivalries and build trust between distant, sometimes competitive leaders. At their best, they bring together all the simple gifts of great organizations:

diverse people with well-stocked minds working together in time and place, with the courage and confidence to disagree. What emerges? Not just solutions but the social capital to make them real.

And hackathons surface leaders. These aren't identified by titles or status. They are the people who emerge from just cultures, thinking for themselves. Once you accept that everyone has gifts, leaders pop up everywhere. They don't just get work done, they think about how it gets done, whether it needs to get done, and what would make it better. They think with others and say what they think, are prepared to listen and open to change. This is easier to do when you have a rich experience of life, the ability to hear, the time to concentrate, a well-stocked mind for reference, and the social capital to be heard. These kinds of leaders know that they succeed when they make others successful and that their shared success, the joy, vigor, and devotion it inspires, persists and is renewed beyond measure.

The alert reader may, by now, have identified some contradictions intrinsic to building a robust culture: you need rest but a well-stocked mind. Focus and attention are vital but so is getting out into the world and walking around. Expertise and knowledge matter but hierarchy is an impediment. You must learn to think for yourself but also with others. Speaking out is important but someone has to shut up and listen.

This book hasn't provided a simple recipe for success; no five habits, six skills, or seven behaviors that guarantee instant achievement. And that is deliberate because business leadership is too complex, beset by too many contingencies, to be reduced to an instruction manual. Those who seek one grow in frustration; those who embrace the dynamic grow in themselves. Organizations are systems, not subject to silver bullets but responsive to just cultures that touch everyone. Recognizing that we need both noise and silence, time for reflection but also for action, the capacity to see the potential in every individual while building up our own store of knowledge, ultimately yields the adaptive minds that respond to change with vigor and integrity.

It's easy to imagine—and some might hope—that all of this might soon become irrelevant. Algorithms are replacing much human labor and will eliminate more. They produce efficiencies but they don't have ideas, they cannot respond with warmth and creativity to human needs, and they offer little in the way of social rewards. Eliminating friction is not the same as creating a rich experience. Far better to aim at making the most of what we cannot manufacture: human ingenuity and connection.

Alert minds might also have picked up the hint of a subtext: that while the small changes described here make a big impact on organizations, they equally impact families, networks, and communities of all kinds. Although I write primarily about business, I've never written only about business, because all the work that we do is in and of the world. Indeed, it is when business allows itself to become separate from the social environments in which it operates that real harm occurs. What we need is not a purely efficient division between two worlds but the mental flexibility to live across them. The relationship of business to society is one of the most pressing debates we face today and won't be resolved unless we can accept that each contributes to, and needs, the other. If there is a winner in this debate, we will all be losers.

The aim of a human life is not one that is free of flaws and friction but one that enriches, and is enriched by, others. Similarly, the goal of a great career or organization isn't the elimination of error but a relationship with the world that is renewable because it grows as it gives. And for that you need all the small things that life has to offer: silence and noise, action and reflection, focus and exploration, time, respect, errors, inventions, humility, and pride in the human capacity to think again.

SMALL STEPS LEAD TO HUGE CHANGE.

One More Thing . . .

A Denver resort, seeking to motivate and inspire its customer service team, came up with a simple mechanism. After you've done what was required, ask yourself: What one more thing could I do to make these people happy? In one case, lost walkers were pointed in the right direction—but then also given some snacks and water to keep them going. In another case, a phone operator cataloged all the easy workarounds to recurrent problems. In every instance, employees found that they could always identify one more thing that would make a difference—and that thing was what they enjoyed most, because it was their idea.

So my one more thing is simply to ask: What small change made a big impact on your work? On your culture? Let your mind wander. You'll find it. Then share it.

ACKNOWLEDGMENTS

This book derives from so many relationships, mistakes, reflections, and research over so many years that were I to enumerate them all, the list might prove longer than the book itself. So I'll restrict myself to thanking those who have most recently challenged and provoked my thinking. Chief among these have been the executives I work with all over the world. Watching the problems they confront; sharing the ambiguity, complexity, frustrations, and pleasures of their work is a perpetual privilege, and I'm grateful for the honesty and generosity that has characterized our work together. It has only confirmed my belief that people come into work seeking to make it better.

I'm grateful also to the mentors of Merryck & Co. who have so energetically supported my work and tolerated my often frustrating schedule. Their insights, experiences, and openness always inspire me and I'm lucky to have such a diverse range of warm and brilliant colleagues.

Many of the organizations I work with have been exceptionally open with me and for that I'm always grateful. In particular, I'd like to thank Severin Schwan, Silvia Ayyoubi, Margaret Greenleaf, and Dina Sabry Fivaz; every conversation we've had has given me food for thought. At the University of Bath, Veronica Hope-Hailey and Christos Pitelis have proved excellent challengers and colleagues. Footdown, the Academy of Chief Executives, Arup, and the King's Fund likewise provided an open and honest forum in which to explore ideas, particularly the importance and power of social capital. At the

BBC, I'm indebted to Hugh Levinson, Gemma Newby, and Helena Morrison for their help in investigating the concept of a just culture. Ben Alcott, Scilla Elworthy, Adam Grant, Verne Harnish, Peter Hawkins, Cathy James, Donald Low, and Maria Lepore have been terrific and generous thinking partners. For the very last idea in this book I'm indebted to Cindy Solomon, whose unvarnished insights into corporate life have always been original and bracing. Jenni Waugh showed great patience with people and ideas I hoped would prove fruitful, while Stephanie Cooper-Lande somehow managed to schedule my time so that I could write. And, as ever, I'm indebted to my agent Natasha Fairweather for making the solitary job of a writer not lonely.

This book would never have been written had it not been for the enthusiastic support and encouragement I've received from the formidable team at TED. In particular I'd like to thank Juliet Blake and June Cohen, whose advocacy for my work has meant more than I can repay. And in an age that often celebrates efficiency at the expense of dialogue, I would like to thank Michelle Quint, whose editorial instincts have always been smart and sharp.

Every book rides on the backs of the author's family—and this one more than most. Why Lindsay, Felix, and Leonora tolerated the obliteration of their summer and many weekends I'll never quite know but I hope they feel that, if these things can be measured, it was worth it. They can't fail to know how much I owe them, not just in their patience but in their willingness to listen and to argue.

This book is dedicated to Pamela Merriam Esty, an extraordinary collaborator with the finest sense of zeitgeist I've ever encountered. Anything I know or think about creativity is measured against her gold standard, and being able to work with her has been one of the great joys of my working life.

CHAPTER ONE

Scilla Elworthy's book on her work, *Pioneering the Possible: Awakened Leadership for a World That Works*, relates a lifetime of work in conflict transformation. You can also see her TEDxExeter talk here: http://www.ted.com/talks/scilla_elworthy_fighting_with_non_violence?language=en

That most people prefer to keep their mistakes private was explored by Professor Jan Hagen at the European School of Management and Technology in Berlin: http://reputabilityblog.blogspot.co.uk/2014/11/error-management-lessons-from-aviations.html.

I am indebted to Verne Harnish for his information about the Torres book of mistakes.

Ed Catmull's book, *Creativity, Inc.*, is full of excellent insights.

CHAPTER TWO

Thomas Malone runs the Center for Collective Intelligence at MIT. You can read more about that work here: http://cci.mit.edu. The experiment described can be found here: http://www.sciencemag.org/content/330/6004/686.abstract. More recent research indicates that these findings hold true in online communication also.

Alex Pentland's work is encapsulated in very accessible form in his book *Social Physics: How Social Networks Can Make Us Smarter*. He also did a TEDxBeacon-

Street talk: https://www.youtube.com/watch?v=XAGBBt9RNbc. He has a good article that you can find here: https://hbr.org/2012/04/the-new-science-of-building-great-teams

Richard Hackman spent his life studying teams. A summary of his publications can be found here: http://scholar.harvard.edu/rhackman/publications. In particular, his work with intelligence teams at the CIA is—or should be—an essential read: https://fas.org/irp/dni/isb/analytic.pdf

Also relevant is this article by Diana Coutu about why teams sometimes do not work: https://hbr.org/2009/05/why-teams-dont-work/ar/1

Helpfulness is an increasingly rich area of study. For further reading, any of these will provide insight:

"Organizational Citizenship Behavior and the Quantity and Quality of Work Group Performance," by Philip M. Podsakoff, M. Ahearne, and S. B. MacKenzie: http://www.ncbi.nlm.nih.gov/pubmed/9109284

"IDEO's Culture of Helping," by Teresa Amabile, Colin M. Fisher, and Julianna Pillemer: https://hbr.org/2014/01/ideos-culture-of-helping/ar/1

In addition, Adam Grant's *Give and Take* is an inspirational antidote to the dog-eat-dog tradition of business books.

For the building of social capital, "How to Build a Motivated Research

Group," by Uri Alon, is fundamental. It's for scientists—but since they make their mark by solving hard problems under considerable time pressure, it is valuable to everyone: http://www .cell.com/molecular-cell/abstract/ S1097-2765(10)00040-7. His TED talk also lucidly describes the connection between fear, risk, and innovation: https://www.ted.com/talks/uri_ alon_why_truly_innovative_science_ demands_a_leap_into_the_unknown

CHAPTER THREE

There is now a vast literature on the perils of multitasking. Much is summarized in Chapter 4 of my earlier book, *Willful Blindness*. In this context also, all of the work on selective attention and cognitive limits by Chris Chabris and Daniel Simons is seminal and accessibly presented in their book *The Invisible Gorilla*. More recent research can be found in "Cognitive Control in Media Multitaskers," by Eyal Ophir, Clifford Nass, and Anthony D. Wagner: http:// www.pnas.org/content/106/37/15583. See also "A Comparison of the Cell Phone Driver and the Drunk Driver": http://www.distraction.gov/download/ research-pdf/Comparison-of-Cell Phone-Driver-Drunk-Driver.pdf

In addition, Russell A. Poldrack has written many excellent studies of the competing memory systems of the brain.

There is an equally vast literature on fatigue. Both topics are well explored in *Is Work Killing You?: A Doctor's Prescription for Treating Workplace Stress* by David Posen, MD, as well as in Chapter 4 of *Willful Blindness*. An

important early work is "Sleep Loss and 'Divergent' Thinking Ability," by J. A. Horne: http://www.journalsleep.org/ articles/110604.pdf.

Marianna Virtanen's continuation of work begun with Michael Marmot's study of Whitehall civil servants is found in "Long Working Hours and Cognitive Function": http://aje.oxford journals.org/content/169/5/596.full

Leslie Perlow's study of time can be found here: http://faculty.washington .edu/ajko/teaching/insc541/reading/ Perlow1999.pdf

Our dislike of thinking, and the short amount of time we give to it, is measured in government data (http://www.bls .gov/tus/home.htm#data), analyzed in the scientific paper available at http://www.sciencemag.org/con tent/345/6192/75, and reported here: http://www.washingtonpost.com/news/ to-your-health/wp/2014/07/03/most -men-would-rather-shock-themselves -than-be-alone-with-their-thoughts/

Walking is widely explored as a way of thinking. There is a good TED talk by Nilofer Merchant about walking meetings: http://www.ted.com/ talks/nilofer_merchant_got_a_meet ing_take_a_walk?language=en. Or you can read more in Marily Oppezzo's "Give Your Ideas Some Legs": https:// www.apa.org/pubs/journals/releases/ xlm-a0036577.pdf. The subject is also well explored in Arianna Huffington's *Thrive*.

The benefits of reading literature was explored by David Comer Kidd

and Emanuele Castano: http://www
.sciencemag.org/content/342/6156/377
.abstract

CHAPTER FOUR

The argument against open-plan offices
is wittily marshaled by Maria Konnikova
in "The Open Office Trap": http://www
.newyorker.com/business/currency/
the-open-office-trap

The conference at which I served and
chopped food was organized by Initiatives of Change at Caux. www.iofc.org

CHAPTER FIVE

The Pygmalion effect in the classroom
was first written up here—

https://www.uni-muenster.de/impe
ria/md/content/psyifp/aeechter
hoff/sommersemester2012/schlues
selstudiendersozialpsychologiea/
rosenthal_jacobson_pygmalionclass
room_urbrev1968.pdf—but was also
written up in the book *Pygmalion in
the Classroom*, by Robert Rosenthal

and Lenore Jacobson. The subsequent
study of the Israeli army platoons
can be found here: http://psycnet
.apa.org/?&fa=main.doiLanding&
doi=10.1037/0021-9010.75.4.394

Teresa Amabile has spent a lifetime
studying creativity in children, education, and organizations. All of her
books are worth reading and she has
also done a TEDxAtlanta talk on the
subject: https://www.youtube.com/
watch?v=XD6N8bsjOEE

Studies of the effects of power are
more thoroughly explored in *Willful
Blindness*, but its impact on empathy
is documented here: http://www
.michaelinzlicht.com/wp/wp-con
tent/uploads/downloads/2013/06/
Hogeveen-Inzlicht-Obhi-in-press.pdf

The design ethos at Apple is discussed
in "4 Myths About Apple Design, from
an Ex-Apple Designer": http://www
.fastcodesign.com/3030923/4-myths
-about-apple-design-from-an-ex-apple
-designer

ABOUT THE AUTHOR

Margaret Heffernan is an entrepreneur, chief executive, and author of *Willful Blindness*, cited by the *Financial Times* as one of the best business books of the decade, and *A Bigger Prize*, winner of the Transmission Prize in 2015. Born in Texas, raised in the Netherlands, and educated at Cambridge University, she was a prize-winning producer for the BBC before returning to the US to run multimedia companies. She blogs for the *Huffington Post* and Inc.com, advises business leaders and teaches at business schools around the world. Her website is available at www.mheffernan.com.

The companion TED Talk to *Beyond Measure* will be available for free on TED.com.

James Duncan Davidson/TED

RELATED TALKS

Margaret Heffernan
Dare to disagree
Most people instinctively avoid conflict, but as Margaret Heffernan shows us, good disagreement is central to progress. She illustrates how the best partners aren't echo chambers—and how great research teams, relationships and businesses allow people to deeply disagree.

Simon Sinek
How great leaders inspire action
Simon Sinek has a simple but powerful model for inspirational leadership all starting with a golden circle and the question "Why?" His examples include Apple, Martin Luther King, and the Wright brothers.

Stanley McChrystal
Listen, learn . . . then lead
Four-star general Stanley McChrystal shares what he learned about leadership over his decades in the military. How can you build a sense of shared purpose among people of many ages and skill sets? By listening and learning—and addressing the possibility of failure.

Fields Wicker-Miurin
Learning from leadership's missing manual
Leadership doesn't have a user's manual, but Fields Wicker-Miurin says stories of remarkable, local leaders are the next best thing. At a TED salon in London, she shares three.

Judge This
by Chip Kidd

First impressions are everything, especially when it comes to design. And design is all around us, secretly shaping our world in ways we rarely recognize. Except if you yourself are a designer. In *Judge This*, renowned designer Chip Kidd reveals the hidden secrets behind each of the design choices, with a healthy dose of humor, expertise, and, of course, judgment as he goes.

ABOUT TED

TED is a nonprofit devoted to spreading ideas, usually in the form of short, powerful talks (18 minutes or less). TED began in 1984 as a conference where Technology, Entertainment, and Design converged, and today covers almost all topics—from science to business to global issues—in more than 100 languages. Meanwhile, independently run TEDx events help share ideas in communities around the world.

TED is a global community, welcoming people from every discipline and culture who seek a deeper understanding of the world. We believe passionately in the power of ideas to change attitudes, lives, and ultimately the world. On TED.com, we're building a clearinghouse of free knowledge from the world's most inspired thinkers—and a community of curious souls to engage with ideas and each other, both online and at TED and TEDx events around the world, all year long.

In fact, everything we do—from our TED Talks videos to the projects sparked by the TED Prize, from the global TEDx community to the TED-Ed lesson series—is driven by this goal: How can we best spread great ideas?

TED is owned by a nonprofit, nonpartisan foundation. Our agenda is to make great ideas accessible and spark conversation.